Charles Morgan on Retrievers

Charley Morgan at the National Retriever Trial, Weldon Springs, Missouri, November 20, 1954. *Photograph: Evelyn M. Shafer.*

CHARLES MORGAN

ON RETRIEVERS

Edited by Ann Fowler & D. L. Walters

A B E R C R O M B I E   &   F I T C H , New York

Published by Abercrombie & Fitch, New York
Copyright © 1968 by Abercrombie & Fitch, New York
Library of Congress catalog card number 67–24866
Printed by Clarke & Way, Inc., New York

Contents

Introduction

There are good books on training retrievers for the beginner. They generally give rules and methods which are sound. But as a trainer becomes more experienced, he realizes that a retriever cannot be trained by a fixed set of rules. Every dog is different; each day's training brings up new problems, which need new answers.

Charles Morgan is one of the most experienced trainers in this country, both in terms of years and in the number and variety of dogs he has trained. He also has one of the finest records in Field Trial competition to prove his success. His friends know him to be one of the most modest of trainers. He is always ready to learn something new, try a different method, readjust his thinking.

So we would like to present this book modestly, not as the complete answer to a retriever trainer's prayer, but as a helpful guide. There is much food for thought in it. If the reader can find some part of it, some idea, some pearl of wisdom which is helpful to him, then we are satisfied.

This book is not for the neophyte. It will take a reader with some experience to understand the full meaning of much of it, and to extract the parts that are useful to him, that apply to his dog and his individual problems. Many ideas are presented, some contradictory, and the reader must think them over, be discriminating, and use what is best for him.

We found it impossible to put the various parts into ABC order. All parts of this book are interrelated. Training just doesn't always go in an even step-by-step sequence. So, if the book sometimes seems a bit disorganized, we apologize. But we just didn't want to change too much, for fear of losing some idea, some thought which will prove useful to somebody. The *whole* picture is the important one. The reader would be wise to read and study all the parts on training, including such chapters as "Does A Dog Think?" to understand the author's basic philosophy. The whole picture will help the reader to understand just why certain methods are recommended and others not, and to be aware of the good as well as the bad consequences of any training maneuver.

As much as possible, when discussing any specific training problem, we have attempted to stress prevention. Then the usual methods of cure are given, and finally the extreme methods, to be used only when all else fails.

Along with helping the amateur trainer, we hope this book will help the owners of retrievers to be more understanding of the problems of the professional trainers and handlers. There are some important messages for owners in "Advice to Young Trainers."

Finally, we would like to give thanks to all of Charley's many wonderful friends and colleagues who have given so much encouragement and assistance. We would like to thank Natalie Morgan, the author's sister, for all her work on the manuscript, as well as the loan of pictures and material. We would like to thank David Way for his interest and help in making this book.

Credit is also due the following sources of information: the books published by The Labrador Retriever Club, Inc., the books published by The National Retriever Field Trial Club, Inc., and *A History Of The Chesapeake Bay Retriever*, published by The American Chesapeake Club.

We are grateful to Charley Morgan for the privilege of working on this book.

ANN FOWLER
D. L. WALTERS

Charles Morgan on Retrievers

CHAPTER *1*

Personal History

First Interest in Dogs

When we were children in Lamar, Missouri, we had a dog called "Jop." He was a little, homeless waif our father had brought home from Joplin, no doubt a gift from one of my father's political friends in return for the cheap campaign cigars that my father forced upon him through the years. Jop was a sturdy little fellow and, like all mixed breeds in that part of the country, had a little black and tan hound in him.

Jop soon became a member of the family and quite a leader in the community. There was no Rotary Club there, so Jop quickly organized his own gang. When prowlers wandered far enough from the Missouri Pacific tracks to reach our back yard, Jop was quick to attack. And when some strange dog ventured too close, he was quick to challenge.

I think we were more proud of Jop than any other member of the family. On account of his pedigree, or lack of one, Jop could not compete with the blue-bloods, but in our eyes he was undeclared champion.

He was a versatile little fellow, too. His stands on quail were staunch and true. As a squirrel dog, he had no superiors, and it was always known that Jop could take one sniff at a brush pile and if he passed it up in disdain, you could bet there was no rabbit there. The coon hunters of the town borrowed Jop for coon hunting, but his love for personal combat often meant that what had started out as a congenial hunt with a little light drinking on the side, would end up as a general free-for-all. Inasmuch as Jop was felt to be the instigator of these fights, he had no backers, human or canine, and the fight usually ended with Jop taking on the crowd.

It was a mystery how Jop escaped with his life, but he would always manage to reach his favorite sanctuary under our house, where he licked his wounds and rested his badly bruised body. Neither food nor water

3

could persuade Jop to come out. Among his accomplishments, he was something of a vet. He treated his own wounds, constantly licking them. There were no vets available. The first day he gave himself up solely to the fleas. At the end of the second day, we would hear a noise, and we knew he was alive. A sense of relief would spread through the family, as Jop was dearly loved by us all. We hoped that at the end of the third day Jop would come out, and out he always came, sound and fit.

Jop was never trained, but he seemed to sense at once what it was you wanted him to do, and as long as it did not interfere with his personal liberty, he did it amazingly well.

The day came when father and mother decided that we would move to Joplin. The world crashed in on me when it was decided to leave Jop in Lamar, entrusted to neighbors. It meant many sleepless nights for me to abandon this lovable dog whose friendship and loyalty over the years had been part of my life. No doubt the poor little fellow spent many unhappy hours under the foundation of the house, and going from place to place in bewilderment.

This, I feel, is the real cruelty to animals, to abandon them. Punishing them sufficiently to earn a place in our lives, to become useful, really proves our love for them. But to leave them, I think, is terribly cruel. In those days, dogs were not accepted as prized possessions. But training them to the point of making them useful has certainly helped win the dog a place in our society. With time, he has become highly valued, and so is well taken care of, fine vets and all. The worth of a dog in hunting, to find, retrieve and save game, is well recognized today.

Early Training Experience

The first dog I trained was a Chesapeake, in South Dakota. I had been reading an article about Chesapeakes, a very interesting article, about their hardiness, their coat, and their American ancestry. Then one day a drayman drove into the lumber yard. I asked him what his dog was, and he said she was a Chesapeake. I said that I would like to get a Chesapeake. He said that I could have his, if I could catch her.

Well, I did catch her. I got out my book, I had a book on training, and by the paragraph, I trained her, force trained her, and she turned out to be a fine bitch. Everybody in town hunted with her. I would read a chapter and train a chapter, and she turned out very well. Later, I shipped her to Tony Bliss to breed to one of his fine Chesapeakes, and he liked her so well that he bought her. He liked the way she was trained, so he would ship me a few dogs each year to train. I think that is what started me in professional training. It was something I liked to do, and it gave me a little Christmas money.

Then, in 1935, I went east at the invitation of Tony Bliss, after Mr. Carlisle had shipped over a fine string of Labradors from England and brought over a Scotsman to look after them. I was told to be sure and go over there to watch this boy handle dogs, because he could blow the whistle and stop them, and checkerboard them wherever he wanted to. It was really fabulous, and that was the beginning of the handling of dogs. The Scotsman was Dave Elliot, and that was in East Islip, Long Island.

Early Trials

Among others at the trials, there was Harry Conklin, who trained Sodak Gypsy Prince, and his daughter, Babe Erickson, who used to judge. Gould Remick was active then, and so was Mrs. Remick, and the Burtons, Howsie and Ernest. Jim Cowie was training, and Paul Svane, too. Down in Delaware, Dr. Parrott was quite an authority. He judged often. Jasper Briggs trained for the Harrimans. Old Tom Briggs, Jasper's father, was an early great trainer, and when I left, Lionel Bond trained for Tony Bliss.

But the dean of all the trainers at that time, the one they looked up to and the one they all tried to imitate, was Dave Elliot. Mr. Carlisle had a great string of dogs, wonderful looking dogs and wonderful performing dogs, too. Dave was hard to beat.

In those days, the tests were not too tough, but you had to go through live decoys, and you had to train your dogs on shot birds, or dead birds; you could not train them on shackled birds. Once I got short of birds, and Tony Bliss said to work the dogs on shackled birds, since we were short of ducks. I lost the next trial because a duck, one of the live decoys, started quacking. I never heard a duck make so much commotion. Sodak Gypsy Prince could not resist it. He grabbed the duck, and he was out.

Then they had pheasant drives at Marshall Field's estate. Mr. Field had a game farm, and he would entertain his friends at these pheasant drives. At this particular trial, they thought it would be a good idea to combine the pheasant drive with the trial, and so they did, in the last series.

There were six dogs and six handlers left, and we were put in a line.

They drove the pheasants over the trees in waves, maybe 10 or 15 at a time. Over they'd come, then a lull, and then more pheasants coming over. Pheasants were everywhere. The judge would come to you and say, "There is a pheasant over by that tree, would you get that particular pheasant?" It wasn't easy. It was a perfect staunching test.

In those days if you had your dog staunch, you had it made; that was the big thing. They had terrific staunching tests, and you were never through the staunching tests until the trial was over. In the last series there might be six dogs on line, and three pheasants shot for each dog. If you were number one, you went number one, but if you were number six, you went sixth. You didn't go up to the line, work, and then withdraw as we do now. You waited on line until it was your turn and you honored every dog.

Sometimes the birds were sprung from traps. The dogs walked at heel, the gunners walked at heel, the judges walked at heel, and we all walked together. We didn't know where the traps were, or the ropes to spring them. The birds were sprung as we walked by, and then shot, singles or doubles.

I remember running Sodak Gypsy Prince. I thought I had a trial won, and then he broke on me. When we got back to Bliss's estate, the Scotch groom, Buckham, asked me about it. He said, "What happened to Prince?" I said, "He broke on me." He said, "Where did he break?" I said, "I was in the cover." He said, "Could they see you?" I said, "No." He said, "Why in the hell didn't you kick him?" "Well, I didn't think that was permissible, Mr. Buckham, that's against the rules." "Oh Charley, my boy, you'll learn something about this game." And maybe I have. But I have always tried to be honest without cheating my dogs.

If one dog could not find a bird, another one was sent for it. We called that "wiping the eye," and it was a great thing if you could wipe another dog's eye. You had really done something; it was an opportunity to humiliate the other handler and win extra glory for yourself.

Sometimes they shot birds in very high cover, almost jungles. You could never see your dog. You could not handle him. The crowd was up on trucks, looking over, and they would shout, "Here he comes, here he comes," and that was the first you knew that your dog had the bird, since he was entirely out of sight. That type of cover would not be used today. There isn't any question that we had better hunting dogs then, but, of course, not nearly as good handling dogs.

My first experience with trials in the Midwest was in 1936, when I judged the first trial in Omaha with Gene Whelan. The next year I came back there with a string of Chesapeakes, and I won with Howes Bonnie Laddie, owned by Dr. N. M. Leitch. I remember the last series—or it was supposed to be the last series. A blind was put out, practically down a road, about 50 yards. There was only one dog who completed this test, my bitch Princess Pat, but unfortunately she brought in a dead duck, as was her habit, so no dog completed it, and they threw the test out. When the test was run over, Howes Bonnie Laddie completed it. In handling tests then, there was lots of yelling and waving of arms, lots of casts and refusals, but the only thing that was thought of was to get the bird.

From then on, I pretty much stayed on the road with a string of dog's keeping headquarters in Joplin and going north to Warroad, Minnesota, to train in the summer with Dr. Leitch. At first, I ran practically all Chesapeakes. At one time I had 16 Chesapeakes on the road with me.

Wisconsin

In 1942, I moved to Wisconsin, and won the Country Life Trophy with Sheltercove Beauty, a Golden bitch, and she was the first Field Champion I made.

A little earlier, about 1940, a big, tow-headed boy was running in the Open. He seemed quite self-conscious. I kind of felt sorry for him, so I went out and offered to help him. Well, he won that trial, and I think he has been winning ever since. That was Cotton Pershall.

The next year Cotton went into the Army, and sent the Wallace's Labradors to me. That was my first experience, I believe, with Labradors. In that group there must have been: Black Magic of Audlon, Black Market of Audlon, Firelei's Hornet, and Kiska Pete, whom I got from Elmer LeGear. They won four Derby Stakes that year, taking all four places, two licensed and two sanctioned. I think they finished in the same order every time. In 1944, Black Magic won the Country Life Trophy, and Sheltercove Beauty won the National. Then, in 1945, Magic won the National.

For a period during World War II, I spent some time as a civilian trainer with the Army, in San Carlos, California. Cotton was there, Billy Wunderlich, Dave Elliot, Roy Gonia, and quite a few of the retriever trainers.

In 1950, I won the National with Beautywoods Tamarack, Dr. L. M.

Evans's Golden, a tough, hard-going dog. Tony Berger had started him. They had to break the ice in St. Louis, and they had to keep a motor boat running to keep it open, to keep it from freezing solid again. It was probably one of the severest and roughest trials ever held as far as tough water work was concerned. He won it, I think, principally on his marking ability and his toughness in the water, although he handled well. The water was refused by a lot of fine dogs at that trial. Ed Moore, my partner at that time, had been a great help in preparing for this trial; a fine helper can mean everything.

Following that, I had, at times, The Golden Kidd, Treveilyr Swift, Keith's Black Magic, Bracken Sweep, and The Spider of Kingswere, one of the best Labradors that ever ran. He came close in three or four Nationals, but could never win. Also in 1950, I won the Country Life Trophy with Black Point Dark Tiger, Mr. Pomeroy's dog, trained by Cotton Pershall. And I ran Hot Coffee of Random Lake, who was second to Tiger in Derby points that year, I think. Later, I sold her to Mr. Pomeroy, who presented her to John Olin. John thus got his feet wet, and they have been wet ever since.

Then there was Little Trouble of Audlon, a very stylish dog with terrific hunt, Nelgard's King Tut, one of the better Chesapeakes, and a couple of good Goldens, Georgia Boy and Harbor City Rebel. Nelgard's Counterpoint, a Labrador bitch, broke all records winning the Country Life Trophy in 1953.

But probably the most satisfaction came from winning the Country Life Trophy in 1961 with Rosie, Cream City Co-ed. She won it by the 10th of May, a very short time. She turned two years old on that date. In 1962, she was the youngest dog in the National, and I was the oldest handler. She finished her Championship her first year out of the Derby. Of course, I got a lot of satisfaction out of that, because I was a little older then; I was supposed to be "on the bench."

My Three National Champions

My three National Champions couldn't have been more different. Shelter-cove Beauty was lazy, indifferent, a slow swimmer and not too fast a runner. About all that she did fast was eat. If she was not sharpened up just right she was hopeless, but she had an uncanny way of never making a mistake. She lacked drive and brilliance, but it's hard to beat perfection.

She had brains, and never laid a foot down wrong, though sometimes she was awfully slow in laying it down at all. She had a tremendous record, winning a Derby Championship and the National in two years. She knew how to do it, and did it with as little fanfare as possible. Dr. Evans said she was a great dog because, like a great athlete, she could relax. Instead of calling her slow, you could say she paced herself well; instead of being lazy, you could say she was just relaxing.

On the other hand, Black Magic of Audlon was wild, eager, never stopping, always going. She seemed to be afraid she might miss something. She was 65 pounds of volatile matter, a trim, sleek, fiery bitch with muscles rippling and eyes snapping with expectancy. At first I doubted whether I could ever get her trained to run, even in Junior Stakes. She was a Tallulah Bankhead, dynamic and spontaneous, but nervous and high-strung. Every trip was to a field trial, she thought, and she just boiled over while traveling. She violated every rule of decency between dog and handler. She jumped on me, she pawed me, and she would not stay put. She wanted to be every place at once, except where she should have been. But, between headaches, I loved her. In 1944, she won the Derby Championship, and in 1945, at Shelter Island, N.Y., she won the National with as spectacular a performance as has ever been seen.

The winning of a National lost none of its luster by her victory. There has been criticism that she won a National that did not have many tough handling tests. She was said to be a poor handling dog, and this tag never left her. Under the conditions in many handling tests today, it would have been hard for her to win. But if present-day dogs were run with Mag on tests where marking and hunting were emphasized, her chances would be far better than theirs. It would have been a crime if a dog with her gifted ability to mark and hunt, her tremendous memory, had not won. She did not mark the area, she marked the spot. People used to ask me how I lined her on the second and third birds of a marking test, and I said, "That's easy. I line her where she looks. It just never fails." She did none of that head-swinging, or eye-rolling; she froze, as if on a point, and there was no doubt in her mind. She *knew*, and I never knew her to be wrong. She was not the best handling dog in the world, but in my book she was the best marking dog of all time.

A few years later, this same Doctor Evans from Minnesota wrote to me, "Chuck, I have it. Got the greatest prospect I've ever had: Beauty-woods' Tamarack. He will win the National for you." So I received Timmy, a trim little male Golden, two years old. Yes, Timmy could do it all, and a lot more, too. It was his extracurricular activities that got the best of me. At Oxnard, California, where I winter-trained, he liked to slip off in the tules and hunt for himself, cruising up and down the cattails while I was trying frantically to locate him. Out over a certain distance he was in his Manchurian Sanctuary, he was on his own. How good he could be, and how responsive to handling, as long as he felt you had your hex on him. But after he had slipped beyond that point, he was oblivious to everything except the wild ducks and mudhens, and the exhilaration of being on his own. I would finally catch him and convince him of his mistake, and he might stay convinced until the next day, or maybe two.

He had the courage of a tiger and a terrific love of the water. Nothing slowed him up, neither briars nor ice, and he knew no hesitancy in completing his mission. He even took my chastisements in his stride. This grandson of Sheltercove Beauty had everything but his grandmother's brains. He was obstinate as a mule, set in doing things his own way. In 1950, at the National in Weldon Springs, Missouri, his courage and determination paid off under the most adverse conditions. He not only went where more timid souls would hardly tread, but he flew into the icy water and came out with tail high, ready to go again. He was a little Golden with terrific heart, courage, ability, and the stamina to take a tremendous amount of work. I think he won because he had more guts than any dog running.

My Way to Success

I attribute my success to hard work and close association with my dogs. I have led the life of a real introvert. The door has been closed to everything else. I loved baseball, all sports really. I helped organize the Missouri-Arkansas League, and was President of it. But now, aside from watching a little baseball occasionally, it is all dogs. There is never a minute that I cannot spend with the dogs, even if just for hikes, and I have loved it. Some of your best, most valuable moments with the dogs are on hikes, letting them relax, loosen up, come closer to you for a better mutual understanding.

I think that as a dog man, I am not especially gifted, nor do I have any revolutionary ideas. I go along with the old ideas that have been proven, adding some ideas I might have picked up along the way. My dogs have been, as a rule, fast and happy workers, and I probably tolerate more unruliness, and punish dogs less, than many other trainers. I have been blessed with good dogs and patient owners, two essentials a professional trainer needs to win.

Charley Morgan with his own FC Cream City Co-ed and the Country Life Trophy, which they won together in 1961, Random Lake, Wisconsin. *Photograph: Vern Arendt.*

FC Firelei's Hornet, November 8, 1945, owned at that time by Mr. H. E. LeGear. *Photograph: Percy T. Jones.*

Charley Morgan and (from right to left) Black Magic of Audlon, Black Market of Audlon, Kiska Pete and Firelei's Hornet, at the time these dogs were running in the Derby Stake.

Labrador Retriever Club, East Islip, L.I., New York, October 27–28, 1945. FC Firelei's Hornet returns a bird to Charley Morgan in a blind. Blinds similar to this were frequently used in those days. *Photograph: Percy T. Jones.*

National Retriever Trial, Bourbon, Missouri, December 3–5, 1943. Charley Morgan and the next year's winner, 1944 Nat. Ch. Sheltercove Beauty, owned by Dr. L. M. Evans. *Photograph: Percy T. Jones.*

Black Magic of Audlon, owned by Mr. Mahlon B. Wallace, jr., delivers a bird to Charley Morgan during the National Retriever Trial which she won, Shelter Island, New York, December, 1945. Judges are: Mrs. J. Gould Remick, Mr. B. F. Genty, and Mr. E. Monroe Osborne. *Photograph: Percy T. Jones.*

Black Magic of Audlon, owned by Mr. Mahlon B. Wallace, jr., the winner of the National Retriever Trial, Shelter Island, New York, December, 1945. *Photograph: Percy T. Jones.*

The last series of the 1950 National Retriever Trial, St. Louis, Missouri. The winning dog, Beautywood's Tamarack, owned by Dr. L. M. Evans, delivers a bird to his handler, Charles Morgan, in the blind. Judges on right are Mr. Cliff Overvold and Mrs. Frances Garlock. *Photograph: Evelyn M. Shafer.*

Charley Morgan and 1950 Nat. Ch. Beautywood's Tamarack, owned by Dr. L. M. Evans, on line in a "walk-up," during the 1950 National, St. Louis, Missouri. The other dog on line is FC Timberstone Trigger, owned by Sam Stout. On the left is Mrs. Frances Garlock, a judge. *Photograph: Evelyn M. Shafer.*

Charley Morgan and 1950 Nat. Ch. Beautywood's Tamarack, owned by Dr. L. M. Evans, December, 1950. *Photograph: Evelyn M. Shafer.*

Mississippi Valley Kennel Club, Peruque, Missouri, October 7–8, 1939. From left to right: Billy Wunderlich, Charley Morgan, Sam Sparks, Cotton Pershall and Orin Benson.

Women's Field Trial Club, Westhampton Beach, L.I., New York, November 6–8, 1953. The professional handlers: (standing left to right) Dave Elliot, Al Staudinger, Gil Bergen, Vance Morris, Charlie Kostrewski, Cotton Pershall, Ray Staudinger, (kneeling left to right) Billy Wunderlich, Bud Hedges, Snuffy Beliveau, and Charley Morgan. *Photograph: Evelyn M. Shafer.*

Snuffy Beliveau and Charley Morgan with some of the retrievers they trained. Random Lake, Wisconsin, 1947.

The American Chesapeake Club's Specialty Trial, April 21–22, 1953, Westhampton Beach, L.I., New York. The judges: E. Monroe Osborne and Howes Burton. President E. C. Fleischmann presents trophies to Chuck's Rip Joy, owned by Mt. Joy Kennels, handled by Charley Morgan; FC Gypsy and owner Vincent O'Shea; FC Deerwood Trigger and owner W. D. Hoard, jr.; and FC Bayberry Pete, owned by E. C. Fleischmann and handled by Bud Hedges. *Photograph: Evelyn M. Shafer.*

The Trainers I Have Known

The finest group of real sports I have ever met are the professional dog trainers. Some have given up promising careers in banks or real estate. There are college graduates and men from fine families with high social position who have left good jobs and the promise of a big future to be dog trainers.

I have trained with them in their own localities, to run in trials where they knew the terrain and cover that would be used and the type of tests the judges were likely to set up. In country unfamiliar to me, where I didn't know the judges or their particular likes and dislikes, my fellow pros have laid out the tests in training. I have put myself in spots where a false suggestion could have hurt, where the wrong type of terrain could have been bad, and I could have been messed up. But never once have I received a bum steer. Yet that weekend we would be competing against each other.

What game has a higher degree or grade of sportsmanship? The Bears and the Packers did not practice together before the championship game. The Orioles and the Dodgers did not work out together before the World Series, they scouted each other. And the Bears and the Packers worked out behind closed doors.

I have been connected with a lot of competitive sports, but none that has produced as high and as fine a group of professional sportsmen as the retriever trainers. They work out with you as if they want you to win. Nothing is held back; no type of cover, land, or water, or anything is denied you, while training for their judges on trial grounds you have never seen. Their suggestions can hurt or be of terrific help to you. I have never been told that a batter was a curve-ball hitter when he was really a fast-ball hitter. Their suggestions on tests, or anything, have never been wrong. They have always tried to help me, and when they come here, I try to help them. It is the professional retriever group's code—do all you can for him before the trial, but try to beat hell out of him at the trial, as long as it's fair. You don't try to get his dogs to break on line, you do everything to help him. Sometimes, to be a good sport, you almost do things that will help him win and hurt your own chances. But oh, oh, how badly you want to win yourself!

Sometimes you overdo it. I remember running against Massie's Sassy Boots, 1956 National Champion, with Frank Hogan running him. He was well out in front going into the fourth, and presumably the last, series. I had a yellow Labrador, Ben (Chevrier's Golden Rod), who was well behind, and Boots was well ahead. But Boots was a breaker. If held on line a long time, he might go, and the longer you held him, the more apt he was to go. I had always sent Ben by a preparatory command, getting my arm down and hand out, as if for a line. It was not really for a line, just a preparatory command to keep him from getting so that he would go on his number, or even a little before his number. I had trained him to wait for the arm and the hand extended before he expected the command to go.

This particular time, it meant so much to Boots, so much to Frank, and they were so far ahead, that I sent Ben quick, so that Boots' period of expectancy could be over, and he could relax with no apparent danger of breaking. But Ben was sent unnaturally, and was a little off in his usual fine marking. Then it turned out there was another series, and in this one both Boots and another high dog fell down, and had I followed my normal procedure when I sent Ben, the procedure he was accustomed to, I might have had a chance.

I think this little act of sportsmanship might have forfeited my chances, but it is common practice in field trials. You don't interfere with the other man and his dog.

I have heard handlers accused of sending dogs loudly or with lots of commotion to upset the other dog, but I have always doubted it. When your dog blows up at the last minute it's a terribly frustrating moment, and you are apt to think the wrong thing; you are seeking an alibi.

Also, I have never heard a professional give an amateur a bum steer, even though that amateur could beat him and show him up the next weekend. They are a bunch of wonderful sports. Everybody gets out through the week and helps everybody else, and on the weekend we try to beat each other.

I have trained with the boys in the East, Ray Staudinger, Vance Morris, Bud Hedges, Jay Sweezey, and in the old days, Dave Elliot, Jim Cowie and Gilbert Bergen.

In the Midwest, I have trained with Cotton Pershall, who has qualified more dogs for the National, and made more Champions, than anyone else. And D. L. Walters, who qualified seven dogs in '62 and eight in '63 for the National, an all-time record. His father is a fine bird dog trainer, and his mother is probably the finest force trainer in the country. Also the younger trainers, Tommy Sorenson, Junior Berth, Jake Baird, Del Huffstutter, Billy Voigt, Roger Reopelle, Floyd Hayes, Gene Kirby, Art Maule. And, in the past, Paul Wood, Verlin Stocks, Joe DeLoia, Herb Strand. And that unbeatable trainer, Billy Wunderlich, and that training marvel, Tony Berger, with whom I had the privilege of training before the three Nationals that he won.

In the Far West, I have trained with Roy Gonia, one of the best on bird dogs, springers and retrievers. Also, Snuffy Beliveau, and Ed Minnogie, who gave up an office in the bank to train dogs.

Through the years I have been associated with several trainers who worked with me. The first one was Orin Benson, at McGregor, Pabst and Boalt's Kennels, River Hills, Wisconsin. Orin was in the beginning of his training then. He was a wonderful physical specimen, a fine looking man, a wonderful outdoorsman and hunter, and a fine shot, but he was a little wild and he liked to have his fun. He was rugged and he could take it, and I imagine a lot of trainers who have tried to follow him have fallen by the wayside. He set a fast pace. But now he has settled down and is a wonderful trainer.

The next one was E. J. Whelan, who judged the first trial with me at Omaha. It was the first time I met him. He was originally a springer man, and had been an accountant. He had judged a lot, was a good shot, and a fine dog man.

And then there was Snuffy Beliveau, an old Marine, a rough-and-tumble boy. We used to have our arguments. We were training together in California, and Snuffy thought I was a little easygoing with the dogs, a little too soft. I remember we went over to Thousand Oaks to watch them train the big cats in the wild animal compound. And I marveled at the patience that this trainer showed in training the young cats to get up on the pedestals. I told Snuffy to notice that he didn't hit them, he didn't touch them with the whip. He only fired the gun and maneuvered the chair he carried. Then they turned in the old lions, and we watched them come down the ramp, and they all had sores and scabs on their noses. Snuffy turned to me and said, "Chuck, you see those sores on their noses?" I said, "Yes." And he said, "Well, that ain't due to petting." So Snuffy, in his mind, had won his point—I was too easy. Snuffy went on to be a great trainer and a very fine handler.

Then Ed Moore came. Ed and his daughter Marcella were probably the finest people I ever knew at bringing up and caring for certain types of dogs. They had a genuine love of dogs. Ed has a kennel of his own now, and has some very fine customers.

I remember when Ray Sommers was with me. Ray had guts. We had a big Chesapeake come in, and I had assigned it to another trainer working for me, but he came in and said he wouldn't train that Chesapeake. The dog was too tough, too mean. Ray, who is not very big, said, "Mr. Morgan, I will take him." So I said, "Okay, take him," and then looked out the window to see if he was going to get killed before he even got the leash on the dog. The dog started to go for Ray, but Ray gave him the swing. He started swinging the dog, what we called in the Army the giant swing. When Ray got through with that dog, he was very much subdued and went along very meekly. Ray had trained previously under Willy Knoecker, a great trainer, which is where he learned the giant swing. Ray is a very fine trainer and a hard worker. I can hear his guns being fired from my kennel and know he works awfully hard. He is a real gentleman, very polite, very considerate, and I think he is doing very well.

Al Hibe was here for a while, and he was a wonderful man in obedience work, in basic training. When he got through training a dog in obedience, the dog really knew it.

Jack Robinson used to come out here when he was working in Milwaukee. Sometimes, when I went to trials, he used to stay here on weekends. Jack has his own kennels now, and is a very fine trainer. He will train anything—even otters and lion cubs, I hear.

Then came Junior Berth, Jake Baird and Billy Voigt. Junior Berth compiled a very fine record when he had Neb (FC, AFC La Sage's Neb). I think he and Neb were the team of the year, one year. And Jake has done awfully well with Ike (Dual Ch. Ridgewood's Playboy). He has turned into a very fine handler. These are two great dogs, and they have helped make Junior and Jake; almost like a great football player on a team can make that team great, so a great dog can make the team of man and dog. But Jake and Junior have had to play their parts, too, backed by hard work, long hours, and lots of time.

Billy Voigt, also, has all the earmarks of a fine handler. He did some awfully good work on Dr. Evans' Tingler (FC Beautywoods' Tingler), before he went into the Army.

I would say the success of these trainers who have been with me is due, in the final analysis, to their own hard work, and any help I have given them has only been to help them get started. Whether they succeed or fail is up to them, and if they succeed, believe me, it will be due to hard work, because that is absolutely the first requirement of a successful dog trainer.

The Puppy

How to Pick a Pup

Pick a pup that has good blood lines, so if he turns out well, you will be able to carry on the breeding. I think your mature dog will reflect more of his grandsire and granddam's qualities than his own mother's and father's. So you go back to the third generation rather than the second to get an idea about his inherent qualities. Also, look for conformation, and that includes size; you want all the advantages that go with a big dog when he's mature.

I don't go along with the idea that when you are going to pick out a pup, you go up to the pen and shake it, kick the box, jump up and down, wave your arms, and yell and make faces—the idea that if a pup runs and hides, you don't want him because he is spooky. I don't go along with that, or with the idea that the bold pup who comes up and jumps on the fence, the one who isn't bothered, is necessarily the choice pup. To me, it might indicate sluggishness and stupidity; and of course, the other pup may be a little too shy.

I would pick out the one who shows a quick reaction, a degree of sensitivity and fear, who wants to run away but whose great curiosity and inquisitiveness overcome his sensitivity, so that he just cannot resist his desire to find out what is going on. He cocks his ears, his head turns to one side, a picture of study, and he looks at you intently. He's trying to figure you out, trying to use his head at a very early age.

I would buy on a hunch. I would let my extrasensory perception, if I have any, help me. If I felt like I was throwing the dice for a natural, I would shoot the works and buy that pup, the one who is not too sluggish, or not too timid, and whose curiosity can overcome his sensitivity, who just wants so badly to know what is going on.

15

The First Twelve Months

After I have picked this pup, I would want to keep him in the pack for a while. I think the big thing with young dogs is to give them a lot of freedom. Let them run with abandon on hikes in the woods, over unusual objects and terrain, over logs, around stumps, down gulleys, over ditches and brush piles, so that the unusual becomes the usual. Let them flush a bird, jump a rabbit, and run with a minimum of interference. I think they need a lot of freedom, and a lot of human association and pack association in early life.

They get a certain amount of training, incidentally. They learn what "no" means as the necessity arises to use it, also a fair idea as to "come," but no intensive training to subdue them. I can't go along with early training at only a few weeks of age. When you are dominating them, I think you are giving them a negative complex. You can take a lot out of dogs that you can't put in them. If too much is demanded of a pup, he becomes a confirmed heeler. You want to encourage your pup to get out and hunt, to seek and explore, and find out things for himself. A curious attitude, a seeking attitude, should be developed; initiative and boldness should be encouraged; very little should be subdued. A little wildness, a little outlawry, may be developed in the hopes it can be corrected later, when all the dog's hunting qualities and positive sides are matured, and his potentials brought out.

Dogs are natural retrievers, but they are retrieving for themselves, to take their kill—glove, pigeon wing, hat, shoe, or dried-up rabbit carcass—to their lair in the woods, to eat now or keep for the future. Freedom from punishment and discipline encourages this. I want a pup to emerge from the early learning period as a wild Indian, with the maximum of human association and the minimum of training. When Mrs. Mahlon Wallace sent me Black Magic and Black Market ('45 Nat. Ch. Black Magic of Audlon, and her litter mate Black Market of Audlon), she said she was sending me a couple of wild Indians. Wild Indians they were, and full of hell.

On hikes, I used to carry a pocket full of crunchons, or kibbles. I would give the pack the come whistle occasionally and reward them with a handful of kibbles thrown in the grass when they reached me. The come whistle is, of course, a form of training, but it is not a restrictive form. It's encouragement to do something, rather than oppression not to do something. To build up, rather than tear down, should be the nature of this first training.

Running in a group this way develops a certain amount of competitiveness; it also builds up desire and aggressiveness. The pups should not be petted and coddled too much, or continually babied, nor should fear be implanted in them. They become accustomed to you and accept you with indifference. They do not avoid you; you just become part of their life. This approach may be slow, but the bond of companionship, all-out faith in you, becomes greater, so that later on, when you start giving commands instead of requests, the change is accepted.

You can change a dog's basic character very little. If you start out with one that lacks it, you will end up about the same way. But if a pup has a lot of natural ability and a forceful character, the kind that makes a fine field trial dog later on, and you set out to ruin it, I think you could. The big thing in raising a pup is to let him alone, let him run, go and have fun, find and eat an old dried-up toad—that won't kill him. Don't be continually shouting and yelling at him. Let him find out as much as he can by himself. In this period you are his companion, that's all; let him absorb you gradually, don't force yourself. Let the Almighty be the teacher, and the pup is finding out a lot.

If you have a single pup, and no other dogs for him to run with, the more association with you, and freedom to run along with you, the better. Above all, these early hikes in the woods, in the fields, over ditches, around unfamiliar objects, are developing a feeling of companionship between man and pup. You're his buddy, and later on that is going to help you in being able to teach him to handle, and all of the mechanical things that we have to do today to win a trial. No doubt, to the dog, he is facing a very complicated world. A lot is going to be expected of him.

One thing in raising a dog, the most tragic thing that can be done, is to raise one alone, devoid of all company either human or canine, cooped up in a small pen. The net result is usually that the pup becomes stir-crazy.

During his early life, the growing pup must have frequent feedings. When people go out and have their fun early in the evening, and feed at three in the afternoon, and then sleep late in the morning, I think that is a starvation period for a pup, and is very detrimental. Pups should be fed the proper food, with vitamins and minerals. Also, be careful about shots and worming; consult a veterinarian about these regularly. It is tremendously important to watch the pup's physical condition in the first 12 months. It is important that a puppy develops well and feels well.

What to Look For in a Pup

What are the things to look for in a pup that make him really worth train-ing? First, sustained interest, interest that builds up. You go out and give the pup a couple of marks, and he is interested even more on the second or third or fourth mark, and his interest keeps getting greater and greater. Black Magic, Sodak Rip, Beautywoods Tamarack, those great dogs that I had were always interested in working. They didn't have many "off" days.

They tell the old story about Cork ('55 Nat. Ch. Cork of Oakwood Lane) breeding a bitch up at Tony Berger's. A pheasant got loose, and Cork got off this bitch, ran out, got the pheasant, brought it back, and finished the mating. To me, that is a great dog, when nothing interferes with or can lessen his interest and excitement in hunting and retrieving birds.

And, of course, intelligence. You see lots of dogs that can run, and they have style, but they can't seem to remember or learn—something is lacking. A dog like that, sometimes, you have to have a long time, and you never do quite realize that he isn't going to make it. You always have hopes for him, don't you? Especially if he has other outstanding qualities, like style and speed.

Look for early memory. The first time you throw a double, and your pup remembers the second bird, this doesn't mean that he's always going to remember the second bird, but it would seem that you're starting with a pup with a good memory. He's a little ahead of the rest. Just keep ahead; it's easier than catching up.

The alert, smart, eager, bold pup, the first time out has a head-start on the sluggish pig, and will, as a rule, keep that lead. Only superior handling, or the eventual development of a dog naturally slower to mature, will change the picture. So, if you are playing percentages, you will not waste your time on the retarded dog unless sentiment is involved or you are accepting a challenge. He who starts out with the best usually ends up with the best.

What makes me decide to wash out a young dog completely, just shelve him for a pet? Complete refusal to do anything, lack of any interest what-soever in birds, being feather-shy, gun-shy, always wanting to walk at heel. Or if he is too timid of human company to want to be with people, or do anything to please people.

This does not mean just a spooky pup. A bright, alert pup should have a tendency to spook. A dog spooks at strange things, and everything is strange to a pup. If it is not too bad or doesn't persist too long, don't let it worry you. A pup that is sluggish and dumb won't spook. Sometimes it is a sign of intelligence, discrimination. But sometimes they are afraid to go out on long retrieves—it's a big strange world. Only age and experience will help, and it takes time to tell if the pup is going to outgrow his spookiness or not.

Now that the demands of training for trials are becoming greater and greater, we are training to a high degree of perfection and some dogs don't quite make it. These are your hunting dogs. We shelve dogs today that we would have kept at one time, but if a dog has some interest and tractability, but not enough drive and speed to strike the eye of a judge, no reason why he can't make a fine hunting dog.

I have had dogs brought to me, that were maybe just pets. The owner doesn't expect much, and if I can only get the dog to go out in the pothole behind the place to retrieve a duck, the owner is happy. Some of the happiest customers I have had are these people, some of the most disappointed people are the ones who didn't win a National.

The big thing is to take it easy. Don't get upset yourself, keep working your dog, and you will have your share of successes. And you will have some failures. Try to get a dog suitable to your temperament. If you expect a perfect retriever and are miserable at any mistake, if you demand a letter-perfect dog and are upset if he is not that, and chances are he never will be that, forget it. Any dog will make you unhappy. But if you like a dog as a companion, can recognize his love and loyalty, can overlook his mistakes to the same degree that he will overlook yours, then by all means have a retriever.

CHAPTER *3*

Early Training

Introduction to the Gun

When I have a group of young dogs out running in the woods, and they are at a distance, interested in something else, have forgotten me, I like to fire a blank and watch their reaction. Maybe one dog will be considerably alarmed, maybe he will show a tendency almost to fade away. That is the dog you have got to be careful with, and later on you will have to handle him with a good deal of caution.

A slight tendency to gun-shyness is almost natural, but when it's serious, it is really a man-made fault, the result of improper introduction to the gun. The potentially badly gun-shy dog should be treated as such early. His introduction to the gun should be very gradual, and every attempt should be made to associate the sound of the gun with pleasure. A blunder at this stage can be very serious.

A man with only one dog can do the same thing. He can test his dog's reaction to the sound of a gun fired some distance away when the dog is interested in something else.

If you do notice a tendency to gun-shyness early, but the dog is crazy about retrieving, there should be no problem in keeping him from becoming gun-shy. It is prevention, rather than correction, that is important here. It is a hard habit to break once established.

The introduction to the gun for a dog that shows signs of gun-shyness should be with food, or with birds if he is terribly birdy, and with a small-caliber gun fired at a distance at the peak of the dog's excitement in the retrieve. The trainer should handle the gun. This is one time when the trainer should not handle the dog; he should shoot the gun way out in the distance, and let his helper work the dog. When the dog is at the apex of his enthusiasm in going for the bird, fire a .22 blank pistol. Repeat this, gradually getting closer each time. If the dog gets a little alarmed, let up

20

and don't advance. When using a blank pistol, remember that the noise comes out of the side, which means that it should be held up higher than normal shooting height. There is a difference in the sound of a blank pistol, a shotgun, and a rifle, and dogs should be introduced carefully to each.

Sometimes, if you are too severe in steadying a pup, you can make him gun-shy. A pup should be as wild as he can be; just let him break at the highest peak of his enthusiasm, and at that point, fire the gun. The average pup will quickly associate the sound with the excitement of retrieving. If the reaction is not good, hesitate, go back a little farther and do it over, until you are finally able to shoot close. This is a gradual process. Later, you can take a shotgun, put out some dizzied pigeons, flush them and shoot them, until you can shoot right beside the dog. With care, you can prevent any dog from becoming gun-shy if he is sufficiently interested in birds and retrieving.

If you get a dog that is already gun-shy, before you invest any time, energy or money in trying to cure him, I would want to be sure that he had enough other good qualities to make the effort worthwhile. I'd want him to be birdy, intelligent, and to like the water, and not to be gun-shy because of a generally sensitive nature, timidity, or spookiness. Also, how severe is the gun-shyness? Does the dog merely move away a few feet, or does he really bolt?

For the dog who is already gun-shy, I have used the old starvation system. I put feed in front of him, and when he starts to eat it, I fire the gun at a distance, just far enough away so that it will stop him from eating. Then, when he retreats, I take the food away from him. The next day I put the food back, and I repeat the process until he reaches a point when he doesn't care, and will go ahead and eat anyway. When he reaches that stage, he is pretty well over his gun-shyness.

And there is the old story of the fellow going out in the boat with the dog and firing the gun. The dog jumps out of the boat, and when he eventually gets tired and comes back in, the man fires the gun again. Finally, the dog gets sick of this and stays in the boat. I don't know that I'd recommend this system.

I think when you are feeding a bunch of dogs, maybe the dinner bell should be a gun. At San Carlos, in the Army, the dogs would hear the food wagon start on its way from the kennels to their area, and it was the sound they were waiting for. When you think you might have dogs whose reaction to the gun is not good, this idea certainly wouldn't hurt.

Introduction to Birds

I like to classify my dogs when they are young: here is a potentially gun-shy dog, or here is one who is bird-shy. I think it is a pretty good idea to find out as soon as possible whether a pup is naturally shy of birds or not. Maybe his first reaction is to crush the bones and eat it, which is an indication of a terribly hard mouth. Of course, that is a dog you're going to have to handle a good deal differently. It is just about like gun-shyness; there are many different degrees of affinity for birds.

The normal early reaction of a dog to birds is to take a bird off into the woods, out of sight even. This is really what makes a dog retrieve; he is not retrieving for you, he is retrieving for himself; you will have to teach him to bring it to you. Well, I would develop that trait and encourage it in the beginning, with hopes of curing the problem later. I don't think you get any good habits in a dog without instilling, in the beginning, some bad habits that have to be corrected later on.

I think the old pack training helps here. Mix in with the group a couple of headstrong, birdy dogs, and let the whole pack chase a wing-clipped bird. Better still, put them in an enclosed field so that the timid ones are kept in close proximity to the bird and the other dogs, and they can't avoid each other. You will be surprised at how quickly, sometimes, the most timid, feather-shy dogs will fall in with the chase.

For the dog that is really feather-shy and absolutely won't touch a bird, I sometimes take a live bird and let it stay in his pen a day. Maybe the dog will be at one end of the pen, and the bird at the other. The dog's just scared to death, won't have anything to do with the bird. Then, the first thing you know, he will start pawing it and mauling it. But let him make up to the bird of his own accord. Oh my! He has eaten it! Well, what if he has? You are lucky. That is his real reason for retrieving, and you can break him of that later.

With puppies, to help make them really birdy, throw a dead pigeon in their pen to maul and play with. Let them fight over it for a while. Or take them down to the pond and turn a hobbled duck loose, and let them chase it, compete for it. And when they get close to it, fire the gun. You can help avoid two problems this way: feather-shyness and gun-shyness.

But for the dog who is too rough on birds, who shows promise of being a natural bone-crusher, your program should be a good deal different. Get him out of the pack fast when you are using birds. Best to shelve him and forget birds completely, until you are ready to give him a good course of force training. He must be handled with the idea that he is hard-mouthed, and all precautions should be taken to prevent the problem from getting worse. With a little negligence, it can become an incurable bad habit.

Introduction to the Water

Cliff Wallace once paid me a compliment. He said, "Chuck, I have always found that if we want to beat you, we had better do it on land. Your dogs are hard to beat in the water." I told him that during the first few years of my training career I trained practically nothing but Chesapeakes, and the only thing we thought of was water, for that was what a retriever was for. We hardly ever thought of using them for upland game; that was incidental, a little extra cream in the coffee. But the big thing was the water; that was all-important. The big retriever in those days was the Chesapeake, and on the shore around Dover, Delaware, if you asked the natives about a retriever trial, they gave you a puzzled look and said, "Oh, you mean the Chesapeake trial." It was the Chesapeake trial first, and then came the other breeds to make it a retriever trial. Primarily, retriever dogs are water dogs. The basic reason for having them is to retrieve ducks from water, so we should emphasize this. It's the most important phase of retrieving, and water tests, in the end, usually determine the winner in a trial. That's where they are won or lost.

I like to introduce a pup to the water in a pack, when it's warm, and with absolutely no restraint. The first introduction is fun, and relief from the heat. I don't try to urge them, just let them walk along the shore. Better still, go in yourself, or get in a boat and row. Don't urge them, don't fight them, just let it be fun.

Then I let my young dogs chase a wing-clipped duck. They get mob crazy. The bold ones start, the less bold fall in, and the timid ones run the bank. After the chase gets really exciting and the duck comes close to shore, they all dive in, and you have the whole bunch in the water. They never catch a diving duck and, if about to, you can turn an old dog loose at the right moment to pick up the duck. Or, when the pups are beginning to tire, throw out a dead duck as the winged duck dives, and fire the blank pistol as they get close to it. You had better not pick up the duck yourself too often; if the pups always fail, they'll get a defeatist attitude and quit. They must win, hence the dead duck, or the old dog to pick up the live duck.

The chase should end in victory. This is often a wonderful way to get a dog started retrieving, and it's a cure for feather-shy and gun-shy dogs.

A month or more of this wild, unbridled fun and competition will encourage a good entry and, as a rule, discourage any reluctance.

But when you start steadying a dog, and he is forced to stay, to be staunch, the real nature of the brute is determined. You'll find out whether he has real love for the water, or a natural hatred which his original zeal to retrieve made him forget, and which gave you the idea that he loved it. He didn't; he loved to retrieve, was nuts about it to the point where he forgot everything. But when he is held, allowed to cool off, to meditate, his love to retrieve diminishes and his natural dislike of the water, which all early methods could not overcome, shows up, and you have a problem. People come to me and say, "My dog loved the water, now he doesn't. What is the matter?" Well, staunching sometimes has this effect. The dog has had time for thought, the hot mark has left him, and it is almost a cold, cold blind, and he doesn't like it at all, does he? But if he liked the water originally, and his early beginning in the water was right, he'll come back with some degree of love for the water, and a fairly good entry.

However, and this is important, to be a top field trial dog, there comes a time when he must be made to go into the water when he would rather not, and the big problem is to force him. And force him you must! It's the turning point in a dog's life.

But before the water crisis is reached, the pup's introduction to water should be as pleasant and exciting as possible. There should be nothing disagreeable about it. No unpleasantness should be associated with his early experiences in the water. Just make it fun and interesting. Let him break with the pack, wave a dummy around wildly to attract and excite the dog, and when he is thoroughly worked up, yell "fetch" or "get back," and let it fly. This college approach can make staunching a little easier, and it encourages a good entry.

Getting a good, happy entry for a dog who really dislikes the water is probably one of the most difficult things we have to face in training dogs for field trials. With a young dog who is steady and started in his work but is reluctant in the water, I try to paint a happy picture. I like to go into the water with him, like to have him follow the boat. Maybe I go into the water and have him retrieve onto land, or work him in shallow water, or across water just too wide for him to jump. I try to find a spot where the take-off is abrupt, where he can't just walk in, but has to jump in, and I make it so enticing that he will go in. I shoot pigeons across water, short birds, quickies, and send him awfully fast, before he has time to think. Keep it as pleasant as possible, and try to see that no complexes are built up. The water hole is just a place, no different from any other. You can have fun there. You can even enjoy a meal there, feed or bread soaked in bacon grease thrown out into the water.

Introduction to Decoys

I like to introduce dogs to decoys on land, especially in winter. Perhaps it is more necessary up north here, where you have a limited time to get dogs used to decoys. Then I like to start them through decoys in the water when their entry is good, but you don't want to discourage them in any way at all, or have to make any corrections. Perhaps I put the decoys at the water's edge, maybe starting with one and gradually adding others; or I put the decoys out in a group and work the dog to one side of them, gradually bringing him in closer.

Work a young dog through decoys upwind, so that the duck is in his nose. Do this until he becomes thoroughly duck-minded, and you shouldn't have any trouble. Make it a quickie, send him fast, and if he makes a pass at a decoy, the word "no" is sufficient.

But I do think it can be a dangerous situation if you correct a dog too severely at first, if you are in too big a hurry. I have seen inexperienced trainers take a young dog and start pounding him over the head with a decoy for bringing it in. I don't think that is necessary. I have seen dogs who, as pups, apparently were good water dogs, but who were introduced to decoys too quickly and were corrected too severely, and were never good water dogs after that.

I think if a dog gets his nose full of duck, he knows that that is what he is looking for. Then, if he brings in a decoy, ignore it. But try to keep that from happening by starting him out with two or three decoys right along the edge of the shore, so that you can get after him and say "no." Then work him up closer and closer to the decoys, and keep adding more and more.

I did have a very fine dog once, a yellow Labrador who belonged to Binks McGregor, and we were in a hurry. We had to get through the decoys, and we figured if he did it, we could win the Country Life Trophy, because he was some dog. I took a decoy from him and I was pretty rough with him. I tapped his head with one, and it didn't work out. The dog always had a water weakness. We always thought possibly that was it—too rough and too quick. That was in my early days of training, and I think I learned my lesson then.

Now I like to ignore a dog when he first touches a decoy, or first smells a decoy. Let him find out for himself. Maybe say "no," but don't be severe with him. You're trying to keep the picture of the water, and all the surroundings, as pleasant as possible. The first impressions must be happy ones, with no disagreeable associations.

I have seen dogs that probably were made decoy-shy by judges who did not use good judgment in putting out the decoys. Maybe they had two feet of water and six or seven feet of anchor line, and with a wind blowing the dog could hardly get through them without getting tangled. Some dogs are more touchy than others, just as some humans are more ticklish than others, and they scare, they spook, they panic. Some dogs, even older ones, are through when they get tangled up with a decoy in a trial. They are out. And this is due to a bad early association. If Harbor City Rebel or the Golden Kidd got tangled in the decoys, they became almost hysterical. A lot of thought should be used by judges in putting out decoys, about how far apart they should be, and about the right depth of the anchor line.

For a dog who persists in picking up decoys, I have taken a long, light fishing pole and tapped him on the head, saying "no" when he started to pick it up. But this problem can be avoided by a gradual approach. I think that is the secret of all your training—the gradual approach, and plenty of time and patience.

Group Work

When should you start intensive training? It depends on the type of pup you have. They don't all reach their full development at the same time or with the same promise for the future. Some apparently have it, with some it is doubtful, and some you might as well wash out—they will just have to marry rich to get by.

If you are interested in the Derby Stakes, your dog may be started quickly, and if he is born at an unfavorable time, half way through the year, you may have to rush him. He must be tough, or you must make up your mind to give him lots of time and attention, lots of time out of training, when you are just together. You must be just lax enough; not so lax as to let him develop any bad habits.

I have had sensitive pups work in a group, go by their name, and staunch to the gun at six months of age. I also had a Chesapeake, Sodak Rip, who pushed King Midas ('41 Nat. Ch. King Midas of Woodend) for the first National Championship, and who was started at 14 months of age. There is no hard-and-fast rule as to the age to start a dog, for so much depends on his character, what you want him for, and how much time you have available.

Will group work hurt a soft dog? Not always. Sometimes the competitiveness of working in a group works to his benefit. The pup, in his zeal to get the bird, forgets the pressure that is being put on him. He is so anxious to go that he forgets all, and takes discipline much better in the group than when working alone.

If a dog is terribly timid and shy, spooky really, but is competitive and birdy, it may help to work him in a group. Black Magic was almost spooky, but believe me, working in a group she was so eager, so competitive, that she would forget it. And I think it was a wonderful thing for her when I worked her in a group down in Joplin at just a little over a year old. I'd dizzy three or four pigeons and tie rags up in the trees so I knew where they were, and I'd walk with a group of six or seven dogs. I'd make them sit, kick out a bird and shoot it, and then send one dog by name. I had Black Market and Black Magic then, and they were wonderful dogs, competitive and very birdy. Black Magic was one of the greatest marking dogs I ever had, and Black Market was one of the greatest handling dogs.

A dog's reaction to group work, favorable or unfavorable, has to be watched. In some cases, punishment given to any other dog in the group subdues him. If his reaction is bad get him out of there, but he may surprise you, he may not always react as might be expected. A terrific sense of jealousy may overcome all fear of loud voices or threatening gestures.

I still like to work dogs in a group. It makes a dog more familiar with his name, because he won't go on any other name. I have had as many as 26 dogs working in a group, but it is a lot of work for the trainer. When a dog learns that his turn will come, he gets used to group work and likes it. You can start with two dogs, teach each to work on his name and stay while the other works, then increase the number of dogs. Rosie (Cream City Co-ed) started at six months in a group of older dogs. She knew her name, and knew what "no" meant.

With young dogs, some of the same results can be accomplished by staking each dog out on a chain after he has worked, so that he can watch the following dogs work. It builds up his desire and competitiveness. It is not a bad thing to do, and does a terrific lot for some dogs. It puts spirit in dogs where there was none, really brings them to life, wakes them up. Maybe it wakes up the neighbors, too.

Basic Commands

After you have developed all the constructive greed and eagerness possible, and desire along with it, you have truly got a wild Indian, a real bronco. Then start your basic commands. Your dog has picked up lots of bad habits, but you have developed certain qualities that are never to be denied. Maybe your early hikes in the woods have given the unbridled creature at your side an idea what "no" means and what the come whistle suggests. But now you cease to ask him and start telling him.

I'd start this around seven or eight months, depending on the date of birth and when you want to get ready for Derby Stakes. With this mechanical age, and the demanding handling tests we have today, you have to start a little earlier than we used to. I like to teach a pup to heel, come when he is called, sit and stay, and staunch him from there on. Now he is going to school. He's had his fun, been out in the woods and learned the facts of life, and now we are getting down to serious training. You can say his honeymoon is over.

Heel, Sit and Stay   The methods of teaching the basic commands are pretty standard. You walk him at heel, and if you are right-handed it is more natural for you to heel him on the right side. I used to use an old buggy whip and a six-foot leash. You can flick the buggy whip at his nose as you jerk him back with the command "heel." When the dog understands what "heel" means, start sitting him. Use the command "sit," a tweet of the whistle, a tap on the rump, and an upward yank on the leash. Then say "stay," take a step forward, and give a restraining yank of the leash with the word again, "stay."

When teaching a dog to stay, I get in a place where I can slip a long 10-foot leash over a post or a fence behind the dog, still holding the end of the leash in my hand. I sit the dog facing me, and as I start backwards I say "stay" and give him a jerk that pulls him back, away from me. If he starts after me, I say "stay" again and give him a sharp jerk back. I do this until I get to the end of the leash. Finally, I give the come whistle with the command "heel," and let him come to me. I keep repeating this, increasing the distance and the pause until I call the dog to me. If he breaks, I repeat it with the leash over the post again, always ending up with two or three come whistles when he does well and can come all the way without interference.

Come   When calling him to me, I stand on a spot alongside a fence so that the dog cannot walk around me, but must come straight to the side he heels on and sit promptly there. If the dog heels on the right, I stand with my left side up against the fence, so that he can only come to the right side. This is a good system to follow when the dog is learning to deliver; it also prevents the dog from walking around you with the bird, a habit that lots of dogs get into.

If the dog learns this work well in three weeks, do it for three more weeks; we always tend to stop too early. When I first get ready to let the dog off the leash, I just let him drag it. Maybe I first let him drag a six-foot leash, then maybe a two-foot one, so he senses that you still have him under control, and I keep it up until it becomes second nature to him.

Dog is left sitting at A. Trainer stands at B, facing dog. Trainer calls dog to him. Dog is forced to sit on right side of trainer, cannot run around him. If dog heels on left, trainer should stand with right side against fence.

Off Leash   In the first place, before I turn a dog loose off the leash I sting him with a slingshot and marble, and yank him to me as I say "heel." He must associate the *ping!* with the command "heel," and a jerk into my side.

Most of the books you read leave you with the idea that all you have to do after a certain length of time is to let the dog off the leash, and he will do all the work as if he were still on the leash. But he knows where he is. He knows he is loose, doesn't he? And you have to be able to reach out and get him with a slingshot or an air pistol, and later on, at a greater distance, possibly even with bird shot. That mysterious sting, he knows not whence it came. He has figured out the leash, but this has him guessing.

If he runs to the car, or wants to run away, I try to have people there to stop him. I don't try to catch him and lick him for doing that. It is considered poor training to coax such a dog back and then lick him, but I have seen some very poor training practices that have worked miracles. But before I turn him loose, I want him so that "heel" becomes mandatory. He can feel that marble, and he whirls and comes to me. So when I think it is time to turn a dog loose, I like to keep him on leash about three weeks or even a month longer. It's easier to quit too soon than to work too long.

When I know a dog is likely to bolt, I like to get people out in strange territory to get after him and chase him back, but I always get somebody else to do it. I like to take a dog that has a sanctuary, maybe it is the car, or his kennel. I like to use that sanctuary. It gives me an opportunity to get that dog under wonderful control. I remember a dog in River Hills, when I was at McGregor, Boalt and Pabst's, a big Golden. We had our dogs housed in stables there, and he would run to the stables where he felt free. I made up my mind that I was going to work that dog until he would come to me off leash three times at a certain distance, and I would keep lengthening the distance. Often I would get him to obey twice off the leash, and the third time he would go back to the stables. Then I would put him back on the leash, and back to the routine. That must have gone on all afternoon, until, finally, when I quit, after four or five hours work, when I called him by the come whistle, he would obey. Fifteen years later a fellow brought me a Golden, and he said, "I don't know what you did to my Golden 15 years ago, but when I called him, he came." I said, "I know what I did, I almost killed myself." I spent the entire afternoon calling him and getting him out of his sanctuary, the place where he was free, where you couldn't touch him, his cave, and believe me, toward the last, when I would blow that whistle or call his name, you could hear him hit the sides getting out of there. His haven just ceased to be a haven. He knew that he had better come when he heard the come whistle, regardless of where he was.

I just believe that sometimes this five minutes of training, twice a day or once a day, just doesn't do it. Sometimes, contrary to usual good training methods, I think maybe an afternoon of constant drill and repetition will do a job that the dog will never forget.

And I don't think you should ever forget the reward. I think in professional training we sometimes get negligent. Maybe we look upon it as amateurish to give the dog crunchons or reward him with tidbits. It relaxes him, brings the dog and trainer closer together, and develops an intimacy that will help in future training.

Force Training

After you have the dog under a good degree of control, so that he sits and stays for a fair amount of time and comes on command at a distance, and he can do this with you out of sight around a building, where you can peek but he cannot see you, and must rely solely on the sound of your whistle, after he responds readily to all this, start force training him.

What is Force Training? Force training is one of the most misunderstood parts of training there is. It is, as Ray Sommers says, misnamed. It should be called force teaching. It teaches a dog to fetch and hold on command. It is not a brutal or severe form of training. My type of force training is pretty mild. Sometimes you hear people say, "Well, if a dog doesn't like to retrieve well enough so that he will do it naturally, and has got to be force trained, he is not worth training at all." Such a dog will never be a happy worker, is their thought. Well, that is the wrong idea. Sometimes a dog's instincts, for some unknown reason, are only aroused this way, and many force trained dogs become happy, stylish workers. They are just started this way, like cranking a car, and once started they love it and are hard to stop. Often force trained dogs get so enthusiastic about their work that they are hard to staunch. And some of the most eager dogs I have had were the most difficult to force train. I think in time you get a better dog if you force train him. I think it is good, because it gives the dog an ordered mission to perform; the retrieve becomes something in the nature of a duty, an order rather than a request.

Yet, when you have a public kennel, and people bring dogs in for you to train in six weeks, they don't expect much. They only want a hunting dog, and the result is that you don't do things that you really should do. To have better dogs, they should all be force trained, and force trained clear through. But you don't; it takes time. The owner comes out, and after a week of force training, the dog looks worse than when he brought him in. You know that, and you also know that a dog goes through these phases. But the owner says, "Well, I think my wife would like to see the dog." He has some pretense for taking the dog home. It is little Johnny's birthday, and he wants to take the dog home for that, and maybe you never see the dog again. The result is that you become discouraged about giving a dog the complete course. But I think that every dog would be better off, and do better work, if he were force trained.

Methods   There are several different methods of force training, and you can start it in the yard or in a room, and see it clear through, or you can finish later with corrections in the field under more natural conditions. If you have the time, I think it is better to finish it clear through by the force method away from the field. But if you are pushed for time and the dog is pretty biddable, maybe your force training can be very limited. I take the dog into a room and force train him to the point where he will reach down to the floor and pick up the bird or the dummy, or I can lead him to the dummy and he'll pick it up on command. It is not a finished job, but with correction in the field it can become finished, and you can save a lot of time. By starting this way, you can accomplish in a room in one day what it takes two weeks to accomplish in the field.

I like to force train a dog with a light, small, round stick, about two inches in circumference and 12 to 16 inches long, so that you can get your hand a little away from his mouth. Sometimes tape can be wrapped around each end to make it look like a dumbbell. This is to keep the center of the stick about half an inch off the ground, so that the dog has no trouble picking it up.

When I start force training, I like to get right down on my knees, with my arms around the dog so that he can't get away from me and I am close to him. I like pinching the ear, not pulling it—a slight pinch on the flap between the fingernails, until that particular spot becomes sensitive. You put the pressure on very gradually, saying "fetch, fetch." As the mouth opens in protest you slip in the stick. As it gets into the mouth, you stop pinching, stop saying "fetch," and say "hold, hold," keeping the stick in his mouth. Then you say "give" when you remove it. Never shout, never yell, never pinch harder than necessary. At first you might have to open the dog's mouth forcibly with the other hand as you insert the stick. As the stick gets in the mouth, all pressure is released. Some dogs react by gritting their teeth, and you have to pry their mouths open. Each time say "fetch" just as mildly as you can, adding a little pressure on the ear, until he turns back his head in mild protest and opens his mouth. Sometimes you have to pinch and pinch the same spot until it becomes a little tender, and then he'll open his mouth a little faster. But it must be gradual; it must be mild.

The dog soon gets the idea that there is an association between opening his mouth, accepting the stick in his mouth, and getting relief from the pinching. Then he will start reaching for the stick. He senses that this is the way to relieve the pressure on his ear, and he reaches for it. Then you keep lowering the stick and holding it farther away. In three or four days he should be reaching as far as the floor, and in a few more days he will pick it up off the floor.

After the dog will reach to the floor and pick up the stick or dummy at the command "fetch," teach him to hold and carry, come to heel and sit. This must come after the dog goes to the dummy or stick, picks it up on command, and carries it back. At first, he will have to be led by the leash. Try working alongside a fence, so that the dog has to stay on the right side, has to make the right turn, and can't circle you, and you can make him deliver with a half-turn on the side you want him to deliver on.

Some trainers like to use a different method, squeezing the paw, or lifting the leg up under. All methods are based on acts that make the dog uncomfortable, and the discomfort is relieved as the stick is placed in the mouth with the command "fetch," followed by "hold, hold," and finally by "give," "drop," or "leave it."

Other trainers like to use the choke collar. They prefer this because they claim that the association is more with the correction or lesson than with the trainer. That is, the dog doesn't associate the punishment with you as much as with the collar and leash, and they feel that this is less apt to intimidate him. However, some very fine trainers say, "I want the dog to associate the pressure with me. I want him to know it comes from me."

Several Lessons a Day, at short intervals, is the accepted procedure. I believe in three or four daily training sessions. However, I have seen a trainer see it through in one long, bitter session that certainly strained the dog's and the trainer's physical and mental endurance to the limit. This lesson extended long after the dog folded up and the trainer's patience was exhausted. A session of this kind leaves both dog and handler in an emotional state that it takes considerable time to recover from. It's a severe ordeal, and possibly has its advantages if it does not ruin the dog. It is usually brought on more by a loss of temper, rather than as a planned procedure. This is not my method. I believe in a gentle approach, with very short sessions at spaced intervals. However, I have used it on occasion for particular dogs and particular situations, and with wonderful results.

In Texas, Tony Berger and I used to discuss different methods of force training, quick, slow, soft and tough. We never fully agreed with ourselves or each other. One time, Tony had a particularly tough and unreasonable dog. He started out behind the cottage for a pleasant little session. Tony was determined and the dog was determined. As I would come in for a drink or a break, I would glance back to see how Tony was coming. At times it looked like a Texas tornado, a big cloud of dust. Sometimes it seemed that Tony was on top, and at other times the dog seemed to be on top. It was quite a battle, and went on all afternoon. Every trainer has had it happen to him. What starts out to be a pleasant afternoon, a pleasant little training session, turns out to be a major battle. Tempers are frayed, patience is exhausted, and neither side will give in. After hours of exhausting work, the trainer feels that he has violated every sound rule of training and the dog may be ruined. He just did not go according to the book. But what really did happen? Tony did a hell of a good job and had a hell of a good dog. It was more than a good job, it was a great job. After watching Tony on this job and seeing its results, I think perhaps Tony was right. See it through. Maybe it takes more guts, but master or be mastered; don't evade the issue.

The Complete Job   I would say you have done a complete job of force training when, as you say "fetch," the dog's ear starts hurting (or his paw, or his leg, depending on the method you have used), and the pain is not relieved until he has something in his mouth, so that he starts looking around frantically for something to pick up. The dog will go through a phase when he is almost panicky to get something in his mouth, but that's all right; he'll calm down and regain his poise, and then you have really got something. The end result is that you can point to anything and say "fetch," and the dog will grab for it without losing any time or asking any questions. He will hold on to it without dropping it, and will give it up on command.

I think one of the biggest follies of young trainers, one of the biggest mistakes they make, is to go out in the field and grab a young dog by the ears, twist them, yell "fetch, fetch," and jam a dummy in the dog's mouth, all without any build-up or any basic force training at all. Well, 15 minutes or half an hour in a room might have taught the dog what his ears are

being twisted for, but now he doesn't know. So it takes at least a week
under these conditions, and often the dog is intimidated. I have seen dogs
that I think were ruined by it. They don't know what it's all about. A dog
should be trained to the point where you can say "fetch," and he'll reach for
something, before you take him into the field.

Force training is an organized program carried out in a room or in the
yard, not in the field. There is a wrong idea that force training is licking or
beating a dog. I've known people who thought that. But it isn't; it is
teaching them gradually, and I think it is the mildest form of training
there is if you do it slowly, an inch at a time. A good force trained dog
usually has a good mouth, and usually you have an easier job in the field
with him. And when you tell him to go in the water, he goes in the water,
usually.

But it is just like staunching. For a little while a dog may lose something; it isn't so much fun anymore, it isn't a picnic. You are telling him
to do something, ordering him to do something. It is time for meditation,
time for thought. Retrieving isn't just due to a wild hysteria of enthusiasm
that makes a dog forget everything. But once he has accepted it, he'll come
back to his original interest and love retrieving.

And don't forget a fun time, when the dog can be with you, when he is
relaxed and on his own, when he is not constantly being pressurized.
I think that a dog shouldn't have a poor picture of your training sessions
from one end to the other, day in and day out. He has got to have some fun.
We often get lax about this. Maybe we haven't the time, or maybe we are
too intent on the problems, but you can't ignore the importance of it.

Delivering

Sometimes people come to me and say, "My dog gets the bird and won't
come back; he runs away with the bird." First of all, when the dog hesitates in returning with the bird, give him a good drill in heeling on command, yanking him on a long cord. When a dog is thoroughly drilled, you
will find that the command "heel" and the come whistle are more effective
if given loudly just as he reaches for the bird rather than after he gets it.
His response will be much better. Raise your voice only when you are
giving an absolute command such as "heel"; all other commands should
be given quietly and calmly. Then, when an absolute command is given, it
really makes an impression.

Dropping the Bird   If a dog has the habit of dropping his head and dropping the bird at you feet, hold up something and pat your chest. He will pick his head up and will just naturally hold the bird better. Never charge him as he brings the bird in, rather withdraw. Don't hunt him, make him hunt you while you disappear down a winding path, over a ridge, or behind a building.

The Chronic Bird-Bolter   For the chronic bird-bolter, that is, a dog who runs away with the bird, I set up a specific routine. I go back to basic training. First of all, the dog is worked on a check cord in the yard, not retrieving; he learns to come to me on the whistle, and is rewarded. I pick the spot where the dummy will later be thrown and put the dog on that spot. He is held by a helper, the check cord attached to his collar. Then I pick the spot where I will always be to receive the dog and stand there. With the end of the check cord in my hands, I give the come whistle and jerk the cord. The helper lets go of the dog, and I pull him to me. I reward him with tidbits on arrival, and always use the same suggestive cue, like patting my leg or clapping my hands. Sometimes I have the boy give a threatening gesture with the whip as the dog is released. Sometimes, if the dog starts to move in another direction, I sting him with the slingshot and a small glass marble when he is not looking, and at the same time jerk him to me as if nothing had happened. In this drill, never sting him with the slingshot off leash—and don't let him see you do it. Always use the come whistle and plenty of praise, and don't take a belligerent stance. The slingshot and marble should be kept hidden from the dog as much as possible. I keep it up until the dog is returning to me perfectly with the cord loose. I always start the dog in the same spot, and make him return to me in the exact spot where I have been standing.

   Then I have the dog sit at heel with the check cord still attached to his collar and the end of the cord in my hand. The helper throws a dummy to the spot where the dog had previously been left sitting. Just before the dog picks up the dummy, I give the come whistle and hit him with the slingshot. If he starts away, I jerk him with the check cord, sting him, whistle, and then give plenty of praise when he delivers.

   Later on, as he improves, the cord should be free. Let him drag it; just whistle him in and praise him. Eventually you can work him off the cord, but always use the same location. He is "in the groove" here, and he almost returns automatically.

   If his problem is in the water, or across water, go through this whole procedure in the yard until it is perfect. Then put the dog back on a long check cord, and work in clear water so that the cord does not become tangled.

I have taken some habitual bird-bolters and cured them in one session, lasting possibly half an hour or more. They must be on leash, and the stinging must be done as secretively as possible.

But remember, when you teach a dog to do something in one half-hour lesson, he will forget it in another half hour or so. When you get a dog to do something that you consider well worth doing, it's safe to double or triple the lessons. If you have the dog doing his lessons well in a month, give him another month.

Staunching

I think that there can be no set rule for the proper age to steady a pup. I think it depends on when you plan on running him. I don't want to get a Derby dog steady the day before the first trial.

If he is basically steady to his commands, and will sit, stay, come, etc., you can start staunching gradually. Tell the dog to sit and stay and back away from him, tossing the dummy up and down and catching it while saying "no," so that he becomes steady to movements, voices, sounds, and false motions. Then when you are a few feet away, drop the dummy behind you while facing the dog. Always keep yourself between the dummy and the dog, so that you can stop him if he starts. He will be easy to stop if he has been well trained to stay. Best to work in the corner of a fence or in an alleyway, so that he has to run around you to get to the dummy. You can back away 15 feet, drop the dummy behind you, then return to the dog and send him. Keep repeating this, dropping back farther each time, and gradually throwing the dummy at angles to the side. Always keep your eye on the dog, and if he starts, stop him by raising your arm and saying "no."

Introduction To The Whistle   You can teach him to stop to the whistle now. In this mechanical age, you can't start him on the whistle too quickly, but you can start him too harshly. Let him know early that he is to stop at the whistle whatever he is doing. But don't overdo it. After his initial lessons, he will be slow and maybe have a tendency to look at you, but don't be too tough with him, keep encouraging him.

You can keep the pup on a leash and let him drag it. When the throws begin to get long, you can slip the leash over a post so that there is never a chance of his breaking.

Then when you go to the field, work him on a leash at first, and just let him drag it. Finally, when you think he is staunch, go to the breaking cord, a nylon string or a leather shoelace through his collar, so that he thinks he is off the leash but is always under control.

Make It Gradual   My idea of staunching is always to send the dog, not to let him go without being sent, and to increase the length of the pause between the throw and the command as gradually as possible. At first, you send the dog practically while the bird is in the air, always with the command "fetch," or "get back," or his name, whichever you like to use. I like to give the command "fetch," as that becomes a definite command to do something, and is positive and not negative. But you don't just turn him loose. You always give him a command, even if the bird is in the air. It may look as if the dog is breaking, but you are really sending him. Then wait until the bird hits the ground before you send him. Then allow a little pause before the command, and then a greater pause. I think that this is the most sensible form of staunching. If a dog has any natural ability to mark, I think it's preserved best this way. He'll keep his eyes on the bird, never expecting to look around at you, as he's about to be sent anytime. Gradually keep lengthening the pause and the distance that you throw the mark.

Some dogs, when held and not allowed to break, lose interest very fast, and some, if held a reasonable time, lose all interest. So the change from sending the dog before the mark hits the ground to a fairly long time after it hits must be gradual. I think the command should be given as his head starts to turn, or at the first indication of restlessness. Try to lengthen this fixed stare until the dog almost freezes on a point. Get a dog to keep his eyes from straying, so that he's always on the bird or dummy, and you will help him a lot in his marking later. He'll always look at the fall, the mark. If you can do this, you are apt to come up with a good marker.

Sometimes you'll see a dog work who loses interest fast when he is held a little while. Maybe when you turn him loose quickly, he shows a lot of interest, a lot of drive, but as soon as he is held a little, he seems to lose that animation and becomes an entirely different dog. Well, the question then is whether you should keep on giving him quickies indefinitely, letting him go right away, or whether you should hold him. Sometimes I think it is better to hold him and let him just live through that. I think he'll come out of it if he is good, and if he's not, he won't. If you don't, you are just delaying what you have to face up to sometime, anyway.

Keep On The Leash   After you think you have the dog staunch, keep him on a leash or breaking cord a month longer. A dog should be staunch so that the only thing that means "go" is the command, and it becomes second nature for him to wait for this before going. It becomes instinctive. There is only one thing that sends him, and that is the command. Nothing else has anything to do with it. The gun and the bird have no bearing on it; the only thing that sends him is your voice. It's "on your mark, get set, go," and "fetch" is the command to go. If you do this you will save yourself lots of trouble later on, and it may keep your dog from ever getting the habit of looking at you and taking his eyes off the marks.

Staunch your dog by habit rather than by intimidation. If you are too quick, too harsh, sometimes you will have a handler-gazer, a dog who watches the handler rather than the bird. He is handler-conscious rather than bird-conscious. You would like to have your dog reach the staunchness stage with an equal interest in both bird and handler. He should have enough interest in the bird so that his gaze never wavers, and yet his awareness of the handler should never be lost. The master's presence must always be there.

Honor frequently. I hold my young dogs when honoring, in the meantime encouraging them and building up their eagerness for the bird. The idea is not to discourage the thought, but to get them to stay by second nature, by habit. And always make the dog heel with you off line.

Rosie (Cream City Co-ed) never broke on me from the time she was staunched to just before the '63 National, while training at Tony Berger's —and that includes both trials and training. I used to give her staunching tests de luxe, walk-ups with the boys throwing birds as I walked, not even stopping, but continuing to walk as the shot was fired and while the bird was in the air. Occasionally I'd stop and heel her back, maybe keeping this up until five or six birds were used, starting back seventy-five yards or so, and ending up with the last one or two shot from the line right in front of her. If you have the least doubt of your dog's staunchness, attempt this first on leash. I noticed, too, that as I got careless, Rosie got careless. Keep going back to the come, heel, and sit drill occasionally.

The Breaker   For the dog who is already a breaker, who senses it the moment that he is off leash, and just won't be staunch whether you like it

or not, you have to go to the slingshot, the BB gun, or the bird shot pistol.
Of all of them, bird shot in a smoothbore gun or pistol is probably the
safest and most effective, and it isn't a brutal thing. Let the dog break
when a bird has been thrown over a hog-wire fence so that he can't possibly
get to it, and sting him with the bird shot. But this is the court of last resort.
After you think he is staunch, give him at least another two weeks on
leash, give him every benefit of the doubt; make sure he understands what
you are trying to put over before getting rough.

If A Dog Slows Up a little after staunching, don't let it worry you. Some
slow up more than others. Maybe you'll have to give him a little more fun
along the way, relax him by letting him break occasionally with the pack.
Go through a certain build-up, maybe yelling and waving your arms, so
that this kind of breaking won't be associated with or affect his subsequent
staunching. Let the whole pack go. You can't do this too much after you
have spent a month or two months staunching a dog, for you don't want
to undo all that you have accomplished. But, at the same time, the fun and
the enthusiasm can't be kept down too long, can they? They have got to
be built up a little, so you have to let up on the training. I think you should
start out with a little fun and end up with a little fun, and in the meantime,
you must have the ability to say "Bozo, your recess is over. Now let's
go to work." There should be a cue, a definite cue for work, and a definite
cue for the end of work, for fun. When you put your dog up and he's had
a little fun, he's relaxed, the world isn't such a bad spot or so gloomy,
and you're not such a mean guy after all. Just release him momentarily
from the monotonous grind—a recess, a coffee break.

But you certainly have got to be discreet about it. I can't feature this
being done with a dog like Sassy Boots ('56 Nat. Ch. Massie's Sassy
Boots), a dog who was a notorious breaker, a dog you had to watch every
minute, a dog who had enough drive to stand constant training. Other
types of dogs you can let know by your own cue that this is fun time.
"Okay, let's go," you shout, and you wave the duck around in your hands
and yell "get back, get back," and you throw it and let the whole bunch go
in. You don't see a fellow throw a duck at a trial by yelling and shouting
and waving his arms. In other words, this is your cue, your signal for fun.
I think it is a wonderful thing. And sometimes it will bring a dog in faster
to you if he knows that you are going to clap your hands on your sides and
that he is going to get to break now. Some dogs who are slow to come in
will come in much faster. But you have to be discreet and do this not too

much. You are still training, and the detraining moments must not be too frequent—and they must follow a definite cue.

I also like to dizzy pigeons for the dogs, flush them right up in front of their noses, let them see them rise up, and then *bang!* give them quickies. It builds them up.

But if a dog starts out looking like a great trial dog and then loses interest for no reason except for being staunched, and not brutally staunched with the whip or bird shot or any of that, well, I don't know whether reverting or undoing your training is going to help out. But I have tried it, and would certainly try anything. Learn to take things in your stride, keep working the dog as he should be worked. The middle of the road is always the best—never be too harsh, never be too easy.

Double Marks

It's important that you get young dogs started running past the bird boys early, so start close and have the boy throw the bird or dummy farther out, so that the thrower is between you and the bird. The dog will have to go close by the boys and will get an early confidence in them. Also, have the bird boys retire as soon as this confidence is fully established, so that the dog will get the idea of working away from the guns rather than always sucking in to them. It is better for a dog to work out after checking the bird boys. Get him out as far as possible and as soon as possible.

I like to start the first singles using a cross wind, because I think the bird rides out more and gives the dog a better opportunity to mark. It is possibly more inviting to the dog.

Start Doubles Early   Just as soon as I get a pup doing singles, I like to start on doubles awfully quick. It develops his memory early, and he'll rely on his memory rather than on a line. I would like my problem to be keeping the pup from whirling and going for the second bird, having to hold him back rather than to get him to go. I don't believe that I want my dogs to be doing singles well first, or even staunch; I want my dogs to start on doubles almost from the beginning. I want them to be doing doubles before I start staunching. I think memory should come first and learning to line second. I have practically started some of my finest marking dogs on doubles.

I make the double a single operation, with really no delay after the first retrieve. I take the dummy out of his mouth on the way back and don't let him even hesitate in going for the second bird. Maybe the delivery will have to be ironed out later on by taking the dog in a room for a separate drill and working on his delivery with your back in a corner and the dog on a short leash.

When I start a pup on doubles on land, I get in a gateway between two fields. The first bird is thrown in one field, and the second bird in the other. In other words, I stand in the gate of a fence and have a bird on either side. This way, the pup can't possibly switch birds. He has to go by me after he has picked up the first bird and is on his way to the second. Retrieving the two birds just becomes one operation. When the pup has retrieved the first bird the job is only half done, and he's on his way for the other. I just grab the first bird from the pup as he flies by me. I want the big problem to be to hold the dog back on the second bird rather than to have to encourage him to go, and I like to get that over to him at a very early age.

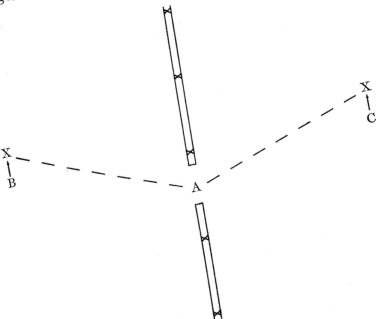

Trainer stands at A in gateway of fence. Bird boy B throws a bird, Bird boy C throws a bird. Dog must retrieve one, and then the other. He cannot possibly switch.

In The Water   I like to start early on doubles in the water, too. Maybe at first you'll have to throw the birds far apart and work the pup on a check cord to keep him from switching. Put the first bird thrown, the memory bird, close upwind so the combined help of sight and smell starts him. You can gradually work the bird into cover, or out of sight behind an island or point.

People often say, always work on fresh ground. But I don't think you should ever do that until the pattern is fully established in a young dog's mind, until he's doing this phase of training instinctively. I like to inch a dog out gradually, but close to the limit of his capacity. Maybe ending up with downwind retrieves, which are the hardest for him, after he's operating well on this pattern. Don't try one thing one day and something else another, a short distance one day, a great distance the next. Make it all gradual, but progressive. If you run into a stone wall, sometimes it is wise to start over again clear from scratch, but try to avoid this.

A lot of people don't agree with me, and want their dogs to do singles well before putting them on doubles. That is the theory, isn't it? But I think if the dog is started right away on doubles, you won't have the problem of his being reluctant to go on the second bird. That problem can be avoided, because he isn't even thinking of quitting when the job is only half done. Sure, you'll have to correct the delivery, but your problem later on will be to stop the dog and keep him from whirling and going right out again, for you have the idea of retrieving two birds before the job is done implanted firmly in his mind.

The Dog Who Doesn't Remember Two   Sometimes I get a dog to train with this problem, a dog who remembers one bird and that's it, he just won't go out for a second bird. Then I have to resort to smell, to sight, or to a line, giving him birds that he can see down a road. I keep walking away from them, getting farther and farther away until he will line down a road for a bird. The next day I'll repeat this training, repeat these lines in the same place, but with the birds in the cover on the wind side of the road, so that when he goes down the road he will wind the birds. The big thing in doubles is to get a dog started. If you can get a dog started he will often react just like a kid, who will scratch his head—"Oh, I remember!"—and then orient himself.

In other words, it all comes back to the dog. The little wheels in the dog's head start functioning, and it all seems to come back after a certain distance. Often you may find that dogs who are started this way have good memories.

Sometimes the refusal to go on the second bird is not due to lack of memory but to harsh or too rapid staunching. The dog is just not sure of himself, and rather than do wrong he does nothing. You can get a dog in this frame of mind by making demands without using the right approach or giving him sufficient explanation. I think success depends on the dog's basic training. If this has been good, the dog learns to realize that there is always a right way and a wrong way. But if dealt with too harshly, they seem to get the idea that there is only one way, and that is the wrong way. They stop trying for the right way. When a dog seeks the right way, you hear the remark, "He is tractable." He has been taught that there is a right way, and you have gotten the idea over that he can please you by finding it.

Memory   Some of the weaknesses in remembering the second bird are no doubt due to a dog's early start. He has been started and kept on long singles so long that he just doesn't seem to grasp the idea of another bird. What determines a dog's memory? As a rule, a dog's memory can be measured by the intensity of his interest, and his lack of memory by a lack of interest. If you are able to get a dog all fired up, excited to the point of insanity, as a rule, he can remember that first bird. So one of the most important things in developing memory is to build up an intense interest, and this cannot be done by too much early obedience, too much negative thinking. To be able to encourage the dog to the point of insanity develops all-out interest. With this type of dog, you will probably have little trouble with memory. The problem becomes one of staunching without taking too much out of him. Do it gradually, so that the maximum of intensity remains.

Another thing to remember, don't tire the dog out before working him on doubles—always try to have him fresh and on edge. See to it that he hasn't already run off his steam in the exercise yard. As soon as he does a fair double, put him up, don't keep working him. If he is tired and spent before working on doubles, you are apt to make little progress. If he is eager and raring to go, he will just remember better. Get him started and it seems to refresh his mind; while on the way out, everything seems to come back to him.

Another thing I do is to use wing-clipped birds. You take these little dogs, they know when a bird is flapping its wings, and that excites them. And the more excited they are, the more the bird is marked in their memory. So give them the winged bird first, the memory bird, then a dead bird thrown out for the second. And let them go fast; it's a quickie. Sometimes that helps, but I'll try everything and anything; sometimes one thing will work, sometimes another. Sometimes, maybe, none of them will work. But it takes a great deal of time. Just be patient and keep working. When necessary, go out and help the dog yourself. One of the biggest mistakes is for the gunners or trainers not to give the dog a chance, to get impatient with the dog, and immediately get the bird thrower to throw up the bird. You can't let the dog roam all over the place or stay out there without doing anything, so, if necessary, walk out and help him yourself.

Forcing On The Second Bird   In an extreme case, when everything else has been tried, a form of force may have to be used. This is most likely to happen in the water, and the dog can be pulled by a long rope, using a boat. I send a helper out in the boat, not a great distance, maybe 20 yards—or he can be on land, across 20 yards of water—and he holds a rope the other end of which is attached to the dog's collar. When I say "fetch," I put my left hand on the rope and give a little jerk, and the helper gives a pull from the boat. And as the dog leaves my side, I give him a touch of the whip across his rump with my right hand. I work him this way until he is responsive to the command to retrieve the bird in the water. Then, when he is going of his own accord, I take off the long rope and put on a short leash, giving him a little jerk with my left hand and a threat of the whip with my right, letting him drag the short leash with him. The motion should be there with both hands each time you send him, a cue with the left to jerk the leash, and a cue with the right as a threat of the whip behind him.

This is a dangerous maneuver and should be done with great caution unless you really know what you are doing. It is dangerous because a dog will panic and fight the rope, and he can tangle and sink. You don't want to be where you can't get to the dog in a hurry, where the pond is too wide or too deep. It can be a very miserable experience for the dog, and much care should be used doing it. It must be done very quietly and calmly, no yelling or beating, and be as mild as possible. It is best done by an experienced trainer.

If you can get in the water yourself, in shorts and tennis shoes, it is fine. it's a much more gradual approach, and not nearly so dangerous for the dog.

On land, a jerk on the short leash with the left hand and a tap on the rump with a whip in the right can sometimes do the trick and get the dog to go for the second bird. I have seen dogs who were stung with bird shot, BBs, or marbles as the trainer said "fetch." But this can be dangerous; sometimes it has repercussions. It is less apt to work out badly if you go another two or three weeks after you think the dog knows the second bird is out there before resorting to real force.

Sometimes the dog who has had to be forced can turn out to be a better dog in the end. I think it pays off for the amount of trouble you have had. The dog goes in the water, and pussyfoots in there, and he looks back, and the only thing you see are the whites of his eyes and his rump floating. It's a terrible picture, it makes you sick. But they gradually ease out, and when a dog gets through, he knows he must go. It may be a long, drawn-out proposition, but when he finally does, you have got him made, haven't you? In this day and age, when so much depends on the water, it is almost necessary. The dog must go; he *must* go; there is just no refusing.

Triple Marks

I have no definite time or age for starting triples. When I have a young dog who is doing pretty well on doubles, occasionally I like to see how he'll do on a triple. In the Derby Stake you can get a few triples, and it is all right once in a while to see if your Derby dog will do triples. Your curiosity will be satisfied, anyway.

If it is not overdone, I do not think triples are detrimental to a Derby dog, but he should still have plenty of singles after he is used to doubles and triples. Almost every workout, I think, should end up with good singles. Start out with a single, then a double, then maybe a triple, and end up with a single. It is a good thing to keep that head from swinging, and to keep his eyes from getting off one bird until he hears the next shot.

Even in early puppyhood, sandwich in occasional triples with your beginning doubles. Give him the idea early that there might be more birds out there, that there is always that possibility, so that he never relaxes completely and feels the job is completed.

When training the young dog, throw another bird out while he is going for the second bird of a double, don't let him see it thrown, and send him out again. In the water, use white plastic dummies so that he can see them easily. Keep sending the pup out 25 to 30 yards after he has retrieved marks. He'll always go for more birds, and won't be reluctant to go for blinds later on. It's always "get back," and the problem is to hold him from going for more. Always train with the future in mind.

I remember old Bayle, the phantom of Lumm's Pond, Vance Morris's Chesapeake. Vance used to give him seven or eight dummies and said he could mark them all. I think he did this when Bayle was pretty young, too.

Maybe it's a good idea to develop a dog's memory, and to develop the idea to keep going back, keep going back for another bird.

Sending Dogs on Marks

I like to send my dogs on the first bird of a marking test by name, so that any movement of my body—lowering the hand, or extending the arm for a line—will not distract a dog's mind or eyes from the bird. I think they mark the first bird better this way, focusing their entire attention on the bird, never leaving it even momentarily. It keeps their heads from swinging, and their minds from swinging, too.

If it is a short bird, they are less apt to overrun it. If you get down and give a line, and maybe your voice is wrong, a little too harsh, and you give them a line as a command and they take it, then *boy!* they can go clean out of the country if they are good line dogs. They'll reach old scents, old trails, and have to be handled in, which is difficult.

If a dog has any tendency to break, however, there had better be a preparatory command. Old Ben (Chevrier's Golden Rod), a yellow Lab, used to be a breaker. He went on his number, and then he got so he would go before his number. So I would stick my hand down, and that was a preparatory command. He knew the command to go was going to come, it alerted him, and he knew then he was going to be sent, but not before. This was a warning.

You develop a cadence, one-two-three: a step, hand down, and "get back." On your mark, get set, go. It is more of a rhythm, and the dog will wait for it. Then, in a trial, you hope he will wait for the hand, the warning signal.

In early training, I like to send a puppy by his name. If I work him out of a group, I have to. Or, if the pup has been well force trained, I'll send him on the command "fetch." That might be all right to use all along. It is a definite order, a command to do something.

Of course, on the second or third birds of a marking test, I use my hand to line out. I try to put the dog in the chute, get him started right, anyway. I figure the second bird, as a rule, is part line and part memory, and the third bird is three-quarters line. A dog is lined out by the direction of your hand and by the direction his body is pointed. If you think it is entirely memory on a marking test, stand facing in the wrong direction so that the dog's body is facing wrong, too. Then send him out by name or by saying, "get back" without giving any hand or arm cast, and see where he goes. I bet he goes in the direction his body is pointed.

The process of putting your hand down, and the one-two-three cadence when sending, can possibly be of benefit in starting a dog on cold blinds later on. It is a build-up to going, and can help to make a more cheerful entry. This preparation will be very valuable later.

Training Problems

Pick-up

When a dog has a poor pick-up, you have a problem that is awfully tough to correct, and difficult even to improve. I have tried to encourage a dog's pick-up by giving him wing-clipped ducks in rushes, where he will lose the bird if he doesn't pick it up quickly.

Another method I try is to turn another dog loose just as the first dog reaches for the bird. You may get good results from this, or you may get bad ones. Sometimes a dog's reaction is, "Oh hell, let him have it," and if that is the way he feels, it isn't going to accomplish anything. Other dogs want to stand over the bird and fight the second dog off, and that reaction is no good either. But if the dog's reaction is to grab that bird, then you can really accomplish something.

Also, try walking the dog on leash by the bird or dummy and, as you walk by, hesitate and say "fetch." The next time, don't hesitate, just say "fetch" and keep walking. Then gradually speed it up—fast walk, trot, until you can *run* by and get the dog to pick up the bird on the run. Theoretically, this is a good system to get the dog to speed up his pick-up, but of course it works only on a dog who has been thoroughly force trained.

As a last resort, you can sting the dog with a marble or BB. But try all other methods first. This is the last thing I would want to do. Set the trap carefully, and be pretty cautious about it.

I knew a Chesapeake, Chesacroft Baron, who had a beautiful pick-up, scooping the bird up on the dead run every time. His pick-up was so fine and unusual that I investigated, and found that he had been stung with a BB and it hit him on the testicles, making a painful wound. It was two weeks before the trainer could get him to pick up a bird after that. He would circle the bird, flare away, refuse it, but he still showed an intense desire to retrieve up to a certain point. Finally, he rushed in one day, snatched up the bird, and fled in wild retreat. He gradually calmed down and became more normal, but to his dying day, at 14 years, he always had a beautiful pick-up and return.

Along the same lines, I knew a trainer who lost with a dog at a trial because he refused the water. On the way home he passed a similar water spot, and he could not resist. He let the dog out, put a blind out in the water, and gave the command "get back." The dog did not move, and he flayed him thoroughly, driving him in. The next day the dog went back to his owner, who ran him at the club trial the next weekend, which he won. I asked him as an afterthought, how did his dog go in the water? He replied, "Oh, with zest; yes, with great zest." So old Baron always picked up his birds "with zest; yes, great zest."

Lots of times, when you accomplish something you can undo something, too, creating a fault that you'll have to correct later on.

It can be a very dangerous thing to let the gunners or bird boys continuously sting a dog for having a poor pick-up. When I went to the Army, I had a dog who was turned over to another professional trainer, and he stung her for her pick-up. Then she wouldn't go out to retrieve any more. She would see a gunner, or somebody, and she was hesitant to go anywhere near. When I got her back, I couldn't get her to go out at all. But she was a glutton for food. So, I used to have fellows come to my kennel, and I'd put guns on their shoulders, and then I'd have them go out and feed her crunchons. When I sent her, she went out to eat; otherwise she would not have gone out at all. It was a funny sight, seeing a bunch of strange people with guns, feeding the dog tidbits. Then, they'd throw out a dummy, and she would run out and get the dummy, and she got so that she wasn't afraid of the guns any more.

Then I went to the water and worked her there. At first she wouldn't have anything to do with the boat, she wouldn't go close to it. But she was a gluttonous eater, and you could overcome anything with her because of her appetite, and I eventually got her over it. Her good appetite and her natural love of retrieving cured her, and she went on to become a National Champion. That was Sheltercove Beauty.

This is a good warning about what can happen in training. She was a pretty intelligent dog, and she knew what was going on—too much so. But all credit must go to the trainer who stung her. He might have made a National Champion out of her by doing that, for her pick-up and return wouldn't have been good enough to have made her a National Champion otherwise. I don't think there is a trainer living who knows exactly what the repercussions are going to be when he tries these things. The better the trainer, the more ways he knows of handling the repercussions. He knows that he has to accomplish *this*, but at the same time, it may cause *that*. He hopes that he can cure *that* later on. That is the secret of training: replace a greater evil with a lesser evil, gradually getting down to fewer lesser evils.

Slow Return

A dog with a slow return represents another annoying problem that is often man-made. The biggest mistake that people make to cause a slow return is to charge at the dog as he's coming in. It almost puts him on the defensive. The object should not be for you to find him as he's running away from you, but for him to find you. Reverse the situation. Go behind a building, out of sight somewhere, so that when he picks up that bird he has to start looking for you. "Where is he? Where is he? Oh, I know! He's behind that building!" Theoretically, he should scoop up that dummy and start looking for you, but it doesn't always work that way. I've seen a lot of amateurs, a lot of novices who obviously were charging at their dogs, going forward to meet them, which is not good.

Incessant encouragement is another possible cause. Sometimes encouragement will speed up a dog, but not always; sometimes it is just the reverse. Don't reward the delivery until it is fully completed. Refrain from giving praise or rewarding the dog until the bird is actually in your hands and the job is done.

Sometimes a poor return is brought on by a trainer trying to force train a dog in the field at the last moment. If there is a hassle every time a dog brings back a dummy or bird—maybe the dog drops the dummy, and day after day gets it slapped back in his mouth—well, the dog may just not care very much whether he gets back or not, because it's going to be unpleasant when he gets there. When you start in the field, keep it pleasant. Give the dog plenty of praise when the job is done—"Nice dog, good dog, here is a crunchon"—and do your force training in a room or somewhere else, before going to the field.

When the dog is older and staunch-proof, so to speak, give him the old break cue as he starts coming in. Swing the dummy around your head, as if you are getting ready to throw it on the break. It usually hurries him up faster, tail wagging and full of animation. As the dog delivers, give a yell "get back, get back," throw the dummy, and open the flood gates— just a good old breaking retrieve, which you started building up to as the dog was returning with his last bird. Patting your leg and waving the dummy might be your cue.

Also, the usual stinging methods can be used. The stinger must neither be too obvious nor too harsh, and it must not be done too much. And with certain types of dogs, it can be dangerous—I don't think you can do it to every dog. Some dogs aren't affected very much, but other dogs are put into a state of fear. A dog is just like a baseball batter. When the batter gets up to bat he must be loose and relaxed, or he can't do a good job of batting. And I think a dog must work with a certain amount of looseness and relaxation. If he is tense, I don't think he can do a good job of marking or hunting or anything. You should try to keep a dog as loose as possible.

But if a dog is puttering around about coming back, and if this is going to ruin him as a trial dog, you must do something. So you try running away from him, you try rewarding him, and you try encouraging him. And when you have tried everything and nothing works, then, as a last resort, you try stinging him. Have somebody behind a tree. Be awfully careful about having the gunners do it. I would have somebody do it who doesn't make it too obvious. He uses a slingshot, *ping!*, while you are standing there looking in the other direction as if nothing were happening. Some people make it so darn obvious where it is coming from that it results in a problem to get the dog to go out and work naturally. Sometimes the only result is that the dog will come in fast if he suspects someone is out there, and if not, he'll revert to his usual slow gait.

I have not been too successful with some dogs I have had, stinging them back. But you hate to see a dog loiter out there, so you tell your boy, "If he lifts his leg, get after him." All in all, your helpers can be more important than you. If they barge in and generate a state of panic and hysteria in a dog, then they are doing more harm than good. Maybe the boy should handle the dog, and you should be out in the field.

With some dogs, it is awfully hard to get a good return. The dog's natural instinct is to get that bird and run back to you with it, but some dogs go into a shell and back-peddle. I think you can help prevent this in early training by retiring yourself and by not charging at the dog.

Hard Mouth

When you first see any signs that a puppy may have a tendency toward hard mouth, that is the time to start preventive measures. If I see a young dog being tough on birds, I take the bird from him, then put it back in his mouth, squeeze his lips to his teeth, and say, "Careful, careful, hold, hold, hold." I make him hold the bird, make him carry it. As soon as his mouth moves, I say, "No, no," and I keep making him carry it. I make him give on command, hold on command, fetch on command—always by command. Long periods of drill, carrying and giving on command, are helpful.

If the problem continues or gets worse, it warrants a licking with the bird. If you see a dog chewing a bird, take it from him, say, "Nice dog," pet him, and then slap the devil out of him with it. Pound his head with it, all the while praising him, saying, "Good dog, good dog." Then jam the bird down his throat and squeeze his lips against his teeth with the bird in his mouth, continually praising him all the while. Make him carry the bird, and if you see him tightening on it, get your hand in his mouth and squeeze his lips against his teeth. But never yell, never shout; don't even raise your voice. I think yelling and screaming at a dog doesn't do any good. It must seem to be the bird that is punishing the dog, so that he thinks it's just that no-darn-good bird that is doing it.

Try to carry this to the point where the bird is not such an inviting, pleasant object after all. When it has reduced itself to a non-delectable state and is just about as tempting to eat as your whip, when it has lost its savor and become an object rather than something edible, and the dog is thoroughly disgusted with the whole procedure, make him carry it some more. It gradually becomes the act of retrieving itself and not the object being retrieved that pleases him.

Then there is the age-old method of having the dog retrieve unpleasant objects with nails in them, birds that have been taped or jacketed with tacks sticking out. A wire harness can be made for a bird, so that the bird can still move and flap its wings and kick. Some dogs want to destroy life. Stilrovin Nitro Express wasn't a hard-mouth dog, but he never brought in a live pheasant; he put the giant squeeze on it and then let up, so that he could never be knocked out of a trial for hard mouth.

When a dog has a lot of other fine qualities but is still pretty tough on birds, I try stinging him with a slingshot just as he reaches for a bird. You can get quick results this way that can get you through a trial, immediate results, but not permanent perhaps. Sometimes you have a last series to go through, and you have to try something desperate at the last minute. You're afraid your dog may squeeze down too hard on a bird, so you go into a neighboring field and throw out a bird, and as he picks it up, sting him with a marble. If the dog knows what he's being stung for, it may enable him to get through the last series.

But, as always, it can get you into problems with a young dog. If he is birdy enough so that he is not going to stop retrieving entirely, or if he does quit and you can get him back, he will probably be a better dog than he was before.

Creeping

I think a creeper isn't really staunch yet. It's the problem of taking the dog off leash too soon. If you have any suspicion that a dog may develop into a creeper, keep him on the leash a month longer, do a more thorough job of staunching. Make the dog sit as quietly as you can with a minimum of effort, and you should be able to avoid the problem. Walk the dog off the line a lot, always at heel.

Try to pick a place where the dog can't creep, maybe next to a ditch or something like that. I talked to a trainer once who had a creeper, and he said he dug a pit in front of the line where he worked the dog, and he camouflaged it, and when the dog crept he fell into the pit. I have never tried that.

I have used hidden mousetraps. Grubby (Beautywoods Chimney Sweep) was the world's champion creeper. He would creep from here to Philadelphia, so I hid mousetraps in front of him. I don't know if they helped or not. I did teach him an awful lot of obedience, an awful lot of heeling on leash. When he started creeping I gave him the whip, always with the same cue, so that he knew it was coming. But I can truthfully say that I never cured him from creeping. I don't know whether I even slowed him up or not.

Some trainers like to use a cue, nasal or oral, which the dog has learned to associate with the whip or with some other punishment for creeping. What happens? They creep in reverse. Little Sam of Woodend would start to back up a few feet, and it was a prelude to a break. I would see a little black object fly by me.

Some dogs are so very different in a trial from what they are in training that it's almost like having two different dogs. On some dogs I have tried everything, including stinging with marbles or bird shot. In a trial, Buck of Monona used to get up on his hind legs and stand, and when he started running on his hind legs, you knew he was going to run on all four of them in a minute. So, what do I do with a creeper? I creep with him.

Once when Martin Hogan was judging, a dog I was handling had run a spectacular trial. He was way out in front going into the last series. Then he rose up on his hind legs, started creeping, and broke. "Why didn't you stop him, Charley?" asked Martin. "It was a shame. He ran such a beautiful trial; he was way out in front." "I'll tell you, Mr. Hogan," I replied. "I just ran out of hisses." Martin Hogan was a stickler for line manners, but he would have liked to have seen me yell or do anything to stop the dog from breaking, for the dog had done such great work. He was entitled to win that trial because of his great work in the field. "Such a pity, such a pity," said Martin, sadly. I have always felt that this was what made Martin Hogan a great dog man. He always wanted to see the best in a dog.

I would say that I have not had too much success in curing a dog who was already a confirmed creeper, but I don't think I have had too many creepers because I try never to let a dog get to that stage. I always try to prevent a dog from becoming a creeper. When I have a dog staunch, I have kept him on the leash a month longer, and have never taken a chance. And in addition, I always honor a lot.

I am not a fender sitter in training. You know, we have fender sitters, they run their dogs, and then they go back and sit on the fender and drink a can of beer. Some of these young trainers are just entertaining themselves, that's all; it's not a training session. But I have always honored, and I think honoring is a big factor in keeping a dog from creeping because you can correct him while honoring in training.

I keep my dogs on the leash a long time in training, and I make them honor. I go up and run my dog, and if someone else is waiting to run after me, I don't interfere with him, but I make my dog honor before I take him off. If he makes a start, I can correct him. Why, I have had more trouble with my dogs backing up than going forward, creeping backwards.

You should solve the problem of creeping early. I believe a lot of bad habits are developed because of hasty, incomplete or harsh training sessions. When the dog is staunch enough to let off leash, keep him on another month. Make him staunch by instinct rather than intimidation.

The Dog Who Is Unruly Heeling to Line

When you have a dog who likes to beat you to the line you can try out-running him, but besides giving the gallery something to laugh about, you seldom win the race. Eventually it becomes a race that the dog enjoys very much, and you always end up coming in on the next train.

In the first place, this situation is brought on by our training, and by letting the dog get into bad habits. It is like creeping—the dog has not been properly trained. In training, we very often work too close to where we park our cars. If we parked our cars 50 yards or more back from where we worked, and if we always made the dog heel properly up to line, we wouldn't have these problems.

Don't try to beat the dog to the line. If the dog starts speeding up, walk slower, maybe make him sit down occasionally. Try tacking and veering like a ship, if the path is wide enough.

A judge once told me to put some wire paper clips on the ends of some light rubber bands, and to let the dog have it in the rear if the need arose while on the death march. Tied to the rubber bands, the clips will come back to your hand. But I think this sounds a little illegal.

Perhaps as a last-minute reminder before going up on line, you could show the dog the chain collar, let him smell the whip, and give him a little nudge in the side or a chuck under the chin. All this is suggestive of an approach, which, in training, has been much more drastic; it reminds the dog of more serious punishment. But in a trial, it is suggestive enough, mild enough and obscure enough, to be permissable.

But these methods can, in time, defeat their own purpose. Instead of subduing a dog they excite him, for he knows that he's about to go on line. The association has changed from one of repression to one of great excitement. It subdues him about as much as saying, "ducks, ducks," animatedly Then you'd better change your approach, or be a little more rough in your training sessions so that those last-minute reminders do not always suggest fun and excitement.

Freezing

Freezing on the bird is certainly one of the most difficult problems to correct. I have seen many fine dogs, with fine trainers, in whom it was never corrected permanently. Temporarily controlled, maybe, so that the dog could get through a trial, but never permanently corrected.

Probably one of the big causes of freezing is encouraging tug-of-war in puppies—it can cause over-possessiveness. Letting a dog swing on an old ring, or hold on to anything, creates a possessive nature. Maybe this is the first step in freezing which, when fully developed, becomes the most difficult of all faults to correct.

In the early stages, a good thorough job of force training may prevent it from ever coming about. Get at it early with constant drill—fetch, hold and give—until the dog spits out the bird on command. Fetch, hold and give, fetch, hold and give, constantly.

With an older dog showing signs of freezing, intensify the sessions. Get him sick of the long, repeated, drawn-out sessions of carrying the bird, until he really wants to give it up.

My advice to somebody with a dog showing the tendency to freeze is to be as calm as possible in training, and to always use the same routine in taking the bird. Make the dog hold it quite a while before you take it. Don't reach down and grab for it; be very unconcerned, very deliberate, very slow, very easygoing.

Avoid pulling the bird from the dog, which is a suggested tug-of-war; a dog should always open his mouth and give on command. You can tell by the way a dog's muscles relax just when you had better reach for a bird, and when you had better not. Or by his eyes—sometimes they get almost bug-eyed.

If it goes on too long and becomes incurable, you will live longer, and the dog will be happier, if you get another dog. But before you are satisfied that he is hopeless, try everything and use anything that works.

Most trainers work out different systems with different dogs until they find the one that is best suited to a particular dog's problems.

The important thing is suggestive training. Billy Voigt worked out a very fine system with Tingler (Beautywoods Tingler). It was suggested by Cotton Pershall, and later carried on by Junior Berth. When she came up to deliver, which he made her do on the right side, he'd reach for the bird with his left hand, pull her up with his right hand by the back of the neck, and then take the bird when she dropped it. Eventually, he'd just let his right hand dangle close to the back of her neck. The dog was conscious of his hand being there at the back of her neck, and she would drop the bird. Of course, in a trial, he could not touch the dog's neck, but his right hand just naturally dangles there when he reaches around with his left hand to take the bird, and that certainly isn't wrong. The dog is used to the hand being there, remembers the training, and drops the bird. Eventually, it does not matter where the hand is, the lesson is there.

I have also tried a quick line to another bird, even if it's an imaginary one. It gets the dog's mind off the present bird and on to the next bird, and he releases the bird in his mouth almost without knowing it. It is not a threatening gesture, and there is nothing illegal about it in a trial. You start doing things on an exaggerated scale and gradually fade, until only the suggestion remains. That's just training, that's all.

Some handlers have used the suggestion of a cigarette or cigar burn while reaching for the bird, merely suggesting it in a trial. But in training, no doubt, it went beyond the realm of suggestion. If it hadn't, it would not even be suggestive at a trial.

Theoretically, these methods or others should overcome the problem, if the dog behaved the same in a trial as he does in training. But they are different dogs, aren't they!

Firelei's Hornet was a freezer of the old school. At a trial, I'd take him behind the car for a drill before I went up on line—fetch, hold and give—and he got so that he would just actually spit the dummy out. Then he would go up on line and do a third-degree job of freezing. I'd try to take the bird from him accidentally, slipping my fingers between his lips so that the lips overlapped his teeth, and putting on a little pressure. I'd take the chance not only of losing the bird, but my fingers as well. It was due to over-excitement, over-possessiveness, probably from early training.

I suggested to Joe Versay that he try this with Boar Ranch Nip when he handled for me once when I was sick. But a friend told me that when Joe returned from the line he was a little pale, a sickly green, and his hand, under his shirt, was oozing blood. Be sure the fingers are between the lips, not just between the teeth.

Some nervous handlers bring on this problem and encourage it by diving at the dog. Sometimes it's pretty hard not to. Here is a dog who comes up on line, you have got the trial in the bag, you have got it won. So you say to yourself, I can take that bird and get it out of his mouth fast, I think I can do it before he realizes what is going on, even before the judges see it, the hand is faster than the eye. So you do it. Fine, you have won a trial. But you know darn well that this is only going to encourage him to freeze harder the next time. You are doing something that is contrary to good training; you would not do this in training.

It becomes quite a game, a tug-of-war that you are suggesting, and it becomes pretty hard not to suggest it. If I am on the line and have got this

Charley Morgan demonstrates his method of force training. Pup opens his mouth when his ear is gently pinched. Trainer gives command "fetch." *Photograph: Walter Mieves.*

Trainer puts stick into pup's mouth, repeating command "fetch." As soon as the pup holds on to it firmly, the pressure on his ear is stopped. *Photograph: Walter Mieves.*

The pup soon learns to reach for the stick with the command "fetch," to relieve the pressure on his ear. *Photograph: Walter Mieves.*

Starting doubles. Charley Morgan reaches out to stop a puppy in the gateway of a fence. The pup has picked up the left bird. Charley takes it. *Photograph: Walter Mieves.*

The pup is on his way to the right bird. *Photograph: Walter Mieves.*

Billy Voigt demonstrates one method of taking the bird from a dog who likes to hold on to it. In training, his left hand takes the bird as his right hand pulls up the back of the dog's neck. *Photograph: Walter Mieves.*

In a trial, the right hand merely dangles over the back of the neck as the left hand takes the bird. *Photograph: Walter Mieves.*

Charley Morgan demonstrates one method of fooling a dog who tends to hold on to the bird. He gives a "false line," so that the dog will think that he is going to be sent for another bird. *Photograph: Walter Mieves.*

dog coming in, and know I have got the trial won, if I am calm and let the dog come in and deliver, drop, and the dog spits it out—well, I have got the trial. But if he doesn't spit it out, boy! I am sunk, I have lost the trial. I could have won by grabbing it, but if I grab it, it means that next time he'll be worse. That is not curing the habit, it is avoiding the cure.

Freezing is something that you can only try to arrest for the time being. You can try stinging with a slingshot before you go up on line. You take the dog out behind the weeds and have somebody sting him as you say "give." Then you go up to the line, the dog brings in the bird, you say "give," and, as a rule, he will spit it out unless he is terribly bad. But as a permanent cure for the dog, this is not good; perhaps it even makes him worse, or develops a bad flinching habit.

Freezing is the most obnoxious and incurable of all faults if advanced too far. You think you have him cured in training, but the excitement of the trial, the excitement of that last series, the importance of it, takes hold of a dog, and he freezes as he never froze before. It is difficult to know who is the most excited, who senses it the most, you or the dog. Maybe a dog has extra-sensory perception on an occasion like this. You have got to be a hypnotist and a darn liar to assume an attitude of complete indifference, an attitude that your dog will not sense.

Whining

I would discourage a dog early from barking or whining on line by scolding and possibly a tap of the whip with "no, no." Judges are more tolerant of this than they used to be. At one time they were so severe that some fine dogs were de-barked by surgery. What happened? The dogs developed an impediment in their breathing that caused them to make a loud rasping, almost choking sound that certainly indicated the dog was in great distress. Discourage whining early, interrupt it, get the dog's mind off the excitement of the present moment.

I like to have a walk-up, and have the boys out maybe 100 yards in front of me. When I start walking, one boy throws a bird to the right, and when he throws that bird, I crack the dog to the ground with the whip, and maybe a hiss, and make him sit as quietly as he can. Then I walk a little farther and have another bird thrown the other way, and again I make him sit as quietly as possible, crack him if he whines, and say "no, no." Then I keep going, and maybe the last bird is shot. When I get to the line, I might even walk that dog back off the line for a third degree of staunchness, for whining, for creeping, for all that stuff. It is just added staunchness and obedience on the line. Then I come back and set the dog down, and at any suggestion of a whine, I crack him with the whip and say "no, no."

Try slapping a dog in the face or across the nose for whining. I think most of your lickings should be suggestive, in the place where it has the most effect. If you want a dog to stop, to punish him for not stopping, hit him across the front legs or chest. If you have to recast him, or are punishing him for not going, hit him across the rear. Along the same lines, hit him over the nose to stop him from whining. You punish a dog where the mistake is made, whether it pertains to the body or the terrain.

To Improve Marking

Little can be done to make a good marker out of a poor marker. It's really a problem of eyes rather than nose. I think all dogs are inclined to be nearsighted. A dog that is farsighted is a better marker, as a rule.

A hunting dog that is allowed to break becomes a good marker. He is chiefly dependent on his eyes; in fact, he is trying to catch the bird before it hits the ground. Oftentimes the untrained hunting dog (the ball-catching dog) does catch the bird. Then he learns that it is second best to find the spot where the bird hit the ground. And finally he finds out it's next best to hit the spot while it's hot and the trail is fresh, and he becomes wise to trailing.

So it is highly important that a dog learn to use his eyes to mark first and second, and learn to use his nose to trail. But it is more natural for a dog to use his nose than his eyes. Unless the value of watching and marking the flight of a bird or object in the air is learned from experience early in life, a dog may never reach his full potential in the use of his eyes, which is essential to becoming a good marker. He'll learn to use his nose and rely on it too soon, and will never become a good marker.

Hell, you say, train them to be good hunting dogs. But to become good field trial dogs, or even superior hunting dogs, we must break down their natural hunting instincts, the inherited characteristics of their forefathers. The dog who hunts naturally must be broken of the habit of quartering before the gun, and broken of the idea that the only place to find birds is

in birdy places—ravines, brush piles, or cover. Keep their retrieves out of
these places; always throw them across or beyond, to teach them hunting
is a lot of boloney. A great hunting dog runs the bank, hunts the shore line,
the marshy places, brush and thickets and all types of cover. To get a good
trial dog, you have to be able to keep him out of these places. Many of the
retrieves in a trial, both marks and blinds, require a dog to go through or
by the natural places for birds and into unnatural places, open water or bare
ground. But be careful; you don't want to destroy his hunting tendencies
completely; you don't want to make a cover-blinker out of the dog.

If you have a good bird thrower, you can help a young dog's marking
a lot. Long heaves or wing-clipped birds flying with the wind off a knoll
will give a long arc that the dog can follow with his eyes from a distance.
The dog is a good marker, isn't he, when his head swings with that arc.
When his head doesn't swing, you know his eyes are not following the
bird. It is important that the bird be ridden out, shot a long way out, or
thrown a long distance from the thrower. I think this habit of throwing a
dummy 15 or 20 feet away from the bird boy is poor. I don't see how a
good marker can stay a good marker under these conditions. A young dog
that gets many shot birds, or wing-clipped birds thrown with long flights
that he can follow, has a far better chance of becoming a good marker, or of
developing all his natural ability to mark.

While I don't think you can take a dog who is a naturally poor marker
and make a good marker out of him, you can take a good marker who is off
his marking and sharpen him up. Maybe the dog has had too much handling,
too many triples or doubles. It certainly is possible to upset a good dog's
marking.

The Head Swinger One of the most important characteristics of a good
marking dog is his ability to follow the flight and fall of a bird without
pulling his head away and looking for another bird to be thrown. The dog
who follows the arc of a bird to the ground and does not switch his gaze
until he hears the next shot, marks and remembers that bird. It has been
engraved in his mind; it is a time exposure.

I like to get the bird boys set up for a triple, and when the first bird
thrower throws a bird and the dog switches his glance at once to the
second bird thrower, I send the dog before the second bird is thrown. (It
is understood that the second bird thrower will hold up his bird unless
signaled to throw.) Then the dog is in a state of confusion and bewilderment. Often he runs in circles, almost as if he had no idea where he was

going. But the next time, the dog should keep his eyes on that first bird, at least until he hears the next shot. Sometimes I make the dog wait a long time. I'm waiting for his head to swing, and when it does, I send him. Doing this two or three times in a training session when he does not follow his birds to the ground will usually help straighten a dog out.

I give doubles and triples a lot in training, but I give more singles. I like to have a double or a triple set up, but give each bird as a single; maybe a single to the right, a single to the center, and then one to the left. This way, the dog is not always anticipating that second bird. It's that anticipation, that looking for the second or third bird, that makes a dog pull his head off a bird before he should.

It can do more harm than good to try and discipline a dog for swinging his head off a bird too soon. It will confuse or excite him, and probably only aggravate the problem because he doesn't understand what it is he is being disciplined for.

Singles   After a dog is doing doubles and triples well, I don't think you can give too many singles to improve or sharpen his marking. He expects a single until he hears a second shot. I like to shoot a few birds from the line and ride them out, maybe into cover or maybe on bare ground where the dog can see the bird, using a white bird so that the dog can watch it. Marking is a matter of the eyes. Send the dog fast, before his mind and eyes start roaming. I think sending fast helps, but of course, you can't keep that up. Gradually lengthen the pause so that the dog will not get into bad habits.

Give quickies at first, sending the dog out with the bird almost in the air. If he is expecting to be sent any second, he will stay concentrated on the fall. Then have the boy throw wing-clipped birds from a high knoll, throwing the bird with the wind and across the dog's line of vision, and get the dog to follow through and swing his gaze with the flight of the bird. Send him fast at first, then gradually lengthen the pause.

Keep your dog guessing. Mix the marks up—short ones, long ones, guns out of sight—and go from quickies, almost breaks, to long pauses. Always send him when his head starts to turn. He will be confused at first, but he will learn to keep his eyes on the bird.

In training we tend to get in the habit of sending our dogs with the exact same pause each time, so that the dog develops a rhythm—one-two-three-go. At that point he is tense, ready, and his mind is right on that bird. Any variation might affect his marking, and if he doesn't get the

command to go then, his mind and eyes are apt to wander. Perhaps we
get in the habit of sending our dogs too fast all the time in training. Maybe
we have visitors who come up to see the dogs work, and we want to make
them look good, so we send them quick. Old Mr. Pomeroy, for example,
came to see his dogs for the first time when I was in Dover. I was sending
them fast, and that old man—he was 85 years old—yelled, "Hey, what
are you trying to do? Make breakers out of my dogs?" He was pretty
keen. If you persist in sending them fast, that is what will happen.

Too often, many of us send our dogs too fast, and just as soon as they
are held, they are in trouble. They mark short, or hunt short, or overrun.
So try to get the dog to hold his concentration on a fall for the maximum
length of time, but always send him when his attention starts to wander.
Gradually get him used to a long wait.

With older dogs who are set in the habit of going past the bird boys
to find the bird, it helps occasionally to have the boy throw the bird in
towards the handler, so that the dog will learn to start looking before he
gets to the guns.

When a young dog starts leaving the area of a fall, allow him plenty
of time to correct himself. Don't be too hasty, consider the area quite
large, and give him plenty of time. Don't interfere with him continually.
This is bad, like interrupting a kid while he is studying; let the dog look
and study a little while. Do you think you are accomplishing anything by
dragging the dog back to the bird and licking him? I doubt it. If the dog
has been properly force trained, scold him, pinch his ear, and repeat the
command "fetch, fetch," as you are leading him back to the area of the
bird. This can help if the dog knows what it means, but he must previously
have been force trained to get any benefit.

But when an older dog goes out and starts puttering around, smelling,
not hunting, he is goofing off. Yell "no, no," run out as fast as possible,
and try to get him in the act. If he has been force trained, grab him by the
ear, pinch it, command "fetch, fetch," and lead him directly to the bird.
Another idea I have seen tried is to pick the dog up and drop him on his
back. Advocates of this system say that nothing humiliates a dog as much,
or brings him down to earth faster—with a bang, no doubt. Or a shot
with .22 bird shot—or no. 8s in the shotgun if the distance is great enough
—will snap the dog out of it. He is daydreaming, and this will wake him up.
However, all this will be done by a dog who lacks genuine interest, and
little can be done about that except, perhaps, better conditioning. Also,
you stand the risk of starting a dog popping, or even coming back to you

without the bird. Too much interference in the field, constant interruption, is not good.

So to improve a dog's marking, try lots of singles, and use birds ridden well out with a long arc that the dog can follow. Vary the distance of the marks, and try to lengthen the pause before sending. Cut out blinds, doubles and triples for awhile. Remember this: after the dog is working well on doubles and triples, emphasize the singles. You can seldom give too many singles to an old, head-swinging dog.

The Dog Who Won't Look Where You Want Him to Go

One of the most annoying habits a dog can have is the habit of looking up at your face or at your hand when you are trying to give him a line. He refuses to look out, either at the bird on a mark, or down the line of your hand on a blind. Possibly it is brought on by a slight touch of hand-shyness; the dog is expecting the hand to do something, or he is expecting the hand to give a signal and will not take his eyes off it.

I have seen dogs take wonderful lines and never look where they are being sent. I don't see how they ever do take a good line, but they do. I try to avoid this problem. It's pretty hard to pull a dog over to you like a magnet once he is in the habit of leaning away from your side, but there are several things you can try to keep the problem from starting.

In the water, I use a lot of white plastic dummies, big ones that the dogs can see easily, to get them in the habit of looking out. They can help on land, too. And sometimes, on triples, I reverse the order of the birds. After the birds are thrown, I turn the dog and take the first bird thrown as the first retrieve, then the second, and third. It is sort of a semi-blind, and it gets the dog used to alerting down your hand.

And I always try to wait until the dog looks the way I want him to go before I send him. I take my time and try to out-wait him. Sometimes it is pretty hard to do; some of them just never do look out. Your good markers always seem to be alert in the right direction, and they naturally look down the line of your hand; the dogs who are looking back at your hand, or up at your eyes, are often the poor markers. And your good line dogs, on a blind, have got to keep looking out. It is the difference between having a feeling of confidence that you can put a dog in the groove, or just guessing, shooting in the dark. In this day of precise lines, it can be the difference between winning and losing a trial.

When I have a dog who is a little soft, maybe one who could easily be a little hand-shy, I try to just reach over and pet him, putting my hand over his head and avoiding any sudden movement, anything that might startle him, anything even suggestive of a slap. I have seen trainers who continually slap the side of a dog's face and get pretty good lines out of him, but I can't see the benefit in that. My idea is almost the exact opposite, to avoid anything resembling a slap. I have even taken some dogs and had crunchons in my hand, to bring them over close to me. But it is pretty hard to pull them over, and if a dog doesn't look out and ahead, it's pretty hard to give him a line.

So use a lot of sight dummies, big white plastic ones that the dog can keep his eyes on; give a dog lots of lines in all directions to dummies that he can see. And try to wait until the dog is looking the way you want him to go before you send him. Wait until he is looking out, down the line you want him to take, or until his eyes are on the bird you want him to retrieve.

Terrain

Remember that a dog's perspective is entirely different when marking from the top of a hill or knoll. Train from a height occasionally, but don't overdo it. Most of your trial grounds are flat, and most marking should be done on the flat.

Too much uphill work tends to slow a dog up. On the other hand, it is a wonderful way of conditioning a dog, hardening him up without making him stale from too much work. Down around Joplin it is hilly country, and my dogs there were in wonderful condition. I think it was from a limited amount of work up and down hills.

Dogs should have a certain amount of work across ridges, through gullies, and in various types of cover and terrain. Also, they should be accustomed to marking against various types of background. In training, a fellow will say, "Get them up, get them up. I couldn't see that, so throw another bird. The dog didn't see that." Maybe it's a good idea to throw a low bird against a bad background once in awhile, one that doesn't get above the tree line. Perhaps the dog will look a little closer, try a little harder, concentrate a little more. And it can be a semi-blind. Help a young dog to get used to going out for something he didn't see.

Use different types of terrain and cover with discretion. Most of your work should be done on the flat, in medium cover.

Trailing

Trailing is certainly of great importance in a shooting dog. You just wouldn't want a dog to hunt with if he didn't trail. Wing-clipped ducks with their feet loose are excellent for teaching a dog to trail. Let the duck walk off a little way, and it is usually a simple matter to get a dog to trail it. I work the shooting dogs in rushes a lot, putting their birds in rushes instead of avoiding them as I do for the trial dogs. And, of course, I do use wing-clipped ducks to help a dog with a slow pick-up.

But it seems to me that trailing, while a wonderful and necessary asset to a good retriever on a hunt, can be bad for a trial dog, and I think it has hurt many a field trial prospect. Even without teaching the dogs to trail, they get on to trailing soon enough, a lot of them too soon. They get to trailing birds, they trail humans, they even trail cars. Some dogs get so trail-minded that they trail everything living with equal abandon. I think trailing can become very detrimental to a field trial dog. It can do him more harm than good.

How can you stop a dog from trailing? You can't. Maybe you can slow it up by moving to fresh ground more often—this is one of the pitfalls of using fouled ground constantly. You can try giving the dog marks and then making him take a line on a blind through the scent of the marks, or you give marks in one direction and then send the dog on a blind, the line to which crosses the lines to the marks.

Wind

Some dogs hate lines or casts into the wind, so that it is almost impossible to keep them going straight into the wind. A dog will usually hold the straightest line going down wind. In a cross wind, he'll fade with the wind to some degree. You generally have to allow for some drift when lining cross wind.

If you send a dog straight into the wind, he is apt to go right or left; he'll quarter back and forth to avoid going directly into the wind.

If a dog really dislikes going into the wind, train on it sparingly. You can overdo training into the wind with a dog who really finds it disagreeable. But don't ignore it altogether. Your training patterns must include lines and casts down wind, cross wind and into the wind, and the same is true for marks.

CHAPTER *5*

Handling

When to Start Handling

A lot of factors enter into the decision to start teaching a dog to handle. Each individual dog is different. It also depends on what you are trying to get out of the dog—do you want him for hunting or for trials? The methods you will use and the dog's individual disposition are as important as his age.

I like to start dogs handling crudely when they are pups. If a pup is having trouble finding the bird, I go out with him. I go out to help him in the initial period, and the wave of my hand and the direction I am going might mean something. It helps me to get something over to him early that will be important later on.

Even earlier, in the pack, when I have them out on hikes, I will sometimes blow the whistle and change direction. They get used to hearing the whistle and expecting to change direction. It's a game, and they learn to love it.

I have seen some good handling dogs who were trained only in the hunting field by wild gesticulations and much waving of the arms by an excited hunter. He yells and shouts and waves his arms, and the dog gets the idea of handling. Odd, how quickly the dogs sometimes catch on to this; they seem to know and understand us better than we know and understand them. No set rule or procedure seems necessary. Novice dog and novice handler are both eager for the same thing, and they achieve a mutual understanding with no system, no savvy, no book learning, just similar desires.

You wonder sometimes at a trial, when—in desperation—you are forced to try and handle a Derby dog who has had no drill or schooling in handling; you are utterly dumbfounded to see the dog handle. More than one experienced trainer has leaned back under these circumstances and said, "Well, I'll be damned!"

But generally I like to see a Derby dog pretty well advanced in his work. If you are not trying for the Country Life Trophy, then I would say to start working on handling before the dog is out of the Derby Stake. Shortly after he is two years old, I believe in concentrating on it. But I do think it affects a dog's marking, so I would lay off the handling until after a dog's Derby career is over if you want a high number of Derby points.

If you have a hard-headed dog, a hard-driving dog, one who is tougher than average, then I would start him handling sooner, and push him a little more. I would be a little tougher with him, and quicker to get on him. But on the whole, try to ease a dog into handling; try to avoid a brawl; go from marks, to semi-blinds, to patterns, until it becomes a habit. Just ease it along.

How to Start Handling; Patterns

My first step, and I think the most important step, is to teach a dog to go "back." After I have taught a Derby dog to be staunch, and he is staunch, I put a bird out in front of him, tell him to "stay," step back behind him, and give him the command "get back." This is the most important command, the one that needs the most constant review. If you are weak on it, it will get you into more trouble later than any other problem. A wrong cast to the right of left can hurt you, but I think a tendency not to take a back cast will probably hurt you more. So I like to have that dominant in a dog's casting; it is his strength. You can place a string of birds or dummies out and walk back as they are retrieved, getting farther away each time as you command the dog to "stay"; leave him, and then give the overhead cast "get back."

In training, if a Derby dog starts coming in to you without the bird, you would say "get back," and drive the dog away from you. I don't like to let a dog get into the habit of coming in; you might end up having to send him out again, a recast. So the first drill in handling should be to "get back."

The old, orthodox baseball diamond drill, as explained in James Lamb Free's book, *Training Your Retriever* (Coward-McCann, 1963), is very good and has helped a lot of people. But I do think it has a weakness, because it tends to make the casts too short. I like to get away from the baseball diamond drill with its short casts, and develop a pattern with longer casts.

There are four casts in teaching a dog to handle: the back cast, right cast, left cast, and the come-in cast. I like to ease a dog into handling, into learning these casts, by starting with marks and then lining back to these marks for semi-blinds. I start with a mark straight ahead, about 150 yards away, then line back to that mark to a dummy at the same spot. Then a mark to the left and a mark to the right, thrown by separate bird boys. In the center, I have a stopping point. When the dog is familiar with each of the lines—straight ahead, right and left—I will line him down the middle and stop him at the stopping point with the whistle.

At first I will have to walk, following the dog out and stopping him with the whistle and a threat of the whip. He should know to sit on the whistle from his yard training, but you will have to follow close and be ready with a threat of the whip to stop him. It may be easier to leave him sitting some distance away, whistle him in, and stop him when he is coming toward you. Each time you stop him, stop him at the stopping point so that he begins to expect it there, so that he is looking for the red light.

Give him a right cast, then a left cast, and always plenty of back casts. There have been marks to the right and marks to the left; the dog remembers them, and will take a cast to the spot he remembers. Make the casts long so that the dog expects to go a long way; get away from short, hacking casts. What was originally a long mark has now become a long blind; the dog has eased into it, and it develops into a pattern.

It takes lots and lots of drill on patterns like this to develop a good handling dog. You can do it in the back 40 or, if you are from Texas, in the front 1,000. We used to have a drill that we did at the airport in Council Bluffs. A bird boy threw a mark down the middle about 150 yards out, then a blind down the middle to the same spot when the dog wasn't looking. Other bird boys threw marks about 75 yards to the right and left of the stopping point, which was about 100 yards out. I'd give the dog a left cast and a right cast, then a left angle line, a right angle line, and a line down the center. Always end up with lines straight to all three points at the completion of the drill—three complete lines, without any stopping.

Maybe your earliest drill in handling could be with this pattern. Leave the dog sitting and back away from him, whistle him in toward you, then stop him with the whistle. Move toward him with a threat of the whip if he doesn't stop. Then give him a back cast, right cast, or left cast to dummies that he has seen being thrown or put out. Walk along with him, so that the direction of your body, your movement, will mean something to him, as well as your arm. Keep reversing your procedure; mix up the casts; but be sure to include plenty of back casts, and end up with three complete lines.

I try to teach definite casts—right, left, back, or come in—and not any so-called "angling" casts. I think that a dog who can do these four directions accurately will have no need for any angling casts. Of course, occasionally, if I want a back cast to the left in a trial, I will give a back cast with my left hand and pivot or step to my left, hoping that the dog will pivot to the left and drift to the left going back. Or I will do the same thing in reverse for a back cast to the right. But I don't train for this. I think a quartering cast is a compromise. You almost have to give contradictory commands—step to the right and say "get back." You do one thing and say another. The dog almost has to compromise. The only drills I ever give are straight back, straight right, straight left, and come in.

Trainer and dog start at E. Bird boy at A throws a mark, then puts a dummy in the same spot (when the dog isn't looking) for a blind. Bird boys B and C also throw marks. After picking these marks up, the dog can be lined back to A, stopped at "stopping point" D, and cast left or right to the dummies that B and C have put out. End up with straight lines to each spot. The bird boys can be removed as the dog becomes familiar with this pattern, and the dummies can then be put out ahead of time. The length of the pattern can be increased.

Remember, your training program should be balanced. Don't get away from any one thing entirely; keep the dog up on his marking; keep his experience active in all areas. And then, don't make your approach too abrupt or too sudden; just ease into the handling lessons, inch out, develop them gradually. Don't go out and try to do blinds or handling tests like the ones you saw in last week's trial with a dog who has just started to learn to handle. Remember, it takes months of work, months of drills and patterns, before the dog understands what it is all about.

It takes months of extended workouts, which will slow up and tire a dog. The fact is, only the trial dogs will survive it. I am a great believer in work, and I seldom agree with the guy who says, "I am going to shelve Old Joe tomorrow, just let him stay in the pen a couple of days, let him think it over. I see the Orioles are coming to town tomorrow, and that ought to be a good series." In my book, it's better to work the dogs out of their problems. I might be wrong, and no doubt have been and will be—but it's too darn easy to shelve your dogs, especially when the Orioles are coming to town, or the Green Bay Packers.

How do I train? I try to start my dogs a little earlier, train them thoroughly to sit to the whistle at heel, then go farther out, gradually lengthening the distance. I have them sit, come in with the whistle, then stop them on the come-in with a threatening gesture of the whip. When I hike with the bunch, I change my direction with a blast of the whistle and a cast, reversing the direction each time. Sometimes with a bunch of young dogs, I throw a dummy with a blow of the whistle. It certainly attracts their attention.

King Tut (Nelgard's King Tut) became a great handling dog this way, and this way alone. He was never shot or prodded in the field—never. He was cast, drilled, over and back, etc. Sheltercove Beauty was a fine handling dog when still a Derby. I ran her in the Open and got a CM because of her handling in the water. She had never been trained to handle in the water, but she took the transition from land to water without trouble. Sheltercove Beauty was never stung or prodded in the field to stop. She was a gluttonous eater, and in the morning I would go to her pen with a pocket full of crunchons. I would open the gate, sit her facing to the right, back up and cast her right; then I would give her a left cast, a right cast, and a back cast; then I'd repeat it; then I would bring her in with the whistle; and then she would get her reward—a crunchon. Then I would repeat the entire drill, casting in each direction. She could hardly wait to come in; it was a terrific game to her. It is usually difficult to bring your dog in with the whistle while hunting, but never "Boots"; she could be brought out of cover immediately, through decoys, off islands. She was one of the few dogs with a lot of hunt who would respond to the come in whistle quickly under any conditions.

Elementary Lines

These days, good lines are all-important. A dog must take the line you give him and hold it. I believe in taking a Derby dog before he is very far advanced in his Derby work, and starting him on lines down a path or road where he can see the dummy. One of the problems we face is getting a dog to take a line cheerfully, or to go into the water on a blind cheerfully. I think that if a dog is started on lining early, you can possibly avoid some of the problems that might arise later on.

I start my young dogs lining down a road, down a ditch, down a corn row, or along a fence. After I can give a dog a line down a road successfully, and he knows where the bird is, then I send him to the same bird but change my own position. One of the weaknesses in our training is that we are constantly moving the birds or the bird throwers, but not ourselves. I think we can change the picture, change the looks of the test, by maneuvering ourselves more. So I give a dog a line down a road, and then I leave the birds where they are and move myself the next time. I move way over to the right or the left to send the dog. I try to move so far over that the dog can't go to the road and then run down it. I move *way* over, and then line the dog back. Don't start trying to give your dogs fine lines, that is, lines very close to the line he has just taken, right away. Move way over, line him back for the bird, and then gradually work closer in toward the road, toward your original line.

Getting a dog to line out with enthusiasm is a problem of deception, and deception is helped by build-up. The dog thinks he has missed something, that a bird has been thrown and is out there, and that he didn't see it. Sometimes you can take a Derby dog who has never had a blind, and give him a line that he takes beautifully; he just thinks that a bird was thrown and he missed it, and he goes with enthusiasm.

But later, when you have to put a little pressure on the dog, and he has time for thought, time for meditation, he thinks it over, and that original enthusiasm sometimes leaves him. Then there comes a time when it becomes absolutely compulsory, a "must"; it is not a "please"; you are not asking, you are telling. And some dogs are like human beings—they almost resent it. Then you will have to put the pressure on. In a dog's life there always comes a time when you have to bear down, when he has to know that he must; and you wonder about the problem of getting him to do it more cheerfully.

Well, I try several things to get a dog to go with more enthusiasm. I take a dog out of the car, let him watch a mark, then put him back in the car and let him wait awhile. When I take him out again, I give him the same build-up as I would in preparation for a mark—"mark, mark," or "get back, get back," or the dog's name, or whatever command he goes on—and then I send him. If that doesn't help, I'll try putting the bird boy out of sight so that it looks as if there is no one there. I build the dog up, "mark, mark," get ready to send him, and suddenly a bird is thrown from behind a hill or a tree, or maybe a bush. The dog wasn't looking for it, and the next time he may think that a bird was thrown out and he missed seeing it—that is where your deception comes in.

If you have a good throwing arm, you can throw a dummy over the dog's head yourself as you send him, or you can throw it when he is about halfway to the distance you can throw. The trouble with this is that some dogs might develop the habit of running out, stopping, and looking back at you, waiting for you to throw a dummy. So don't persist in this too much, and don't let the dog see you throw. This can be a bad habit, like throwing stones in the water for the family pet.

Sometimes, to quicken the start or enthusiasm in taking a line, I have three birds shot and let the dog see them all. Then I put him back in the car for a while and let the guns retire from sight. After a pause, I bring the dog out, give him the old build-up in cadence, "mark, mark, get back," and send him. In the early days, I used to use the same cadence they do in track meets: "On your mark, get set, go"; only I'd say, "steady, hiss, and fetch."

This build-up, this rhythmical approach which has been developed in the course of a dog's training, becomes all-important now. If you can carry right on with it in the blinds, it gives a dog more confidence.

Another suggestion is to give two marks, right and left, and then a mark to center. Pick up the right and left birds and then, before picking up the center bird, repeat the same double, right and left, or give a series of doubles. Then send the dog for the remaining center bird, which has really become a semi-blind.

Sometimes, if a dog is especially birdy, I use live hobbled birds on blinds. Some dogs like ducks much better than pheasants or pigeons, so then I use a hobbled duck. That is the thing that excites him the most; it is his reward; line him up, and there'll be a hobbled duck out there.

In the water, the problem is the same. A dog's enthusiasm will depend a lot on his early introduction to water and his early training in it. Does he have a happy picture, or a miserable picture of the water? It's pretty hard to get a good, happy entry if a dog really dislikes the water, hates it, dreads it. Once again, deception can play a big part. If a dog thinks he's being sent for a mark, it isn't a blind when you send him out; but still, there has to be a certain amount of "must" instilled in the dog. He knows he must, but he enjoys it too. This is a difficult thing to bring about. Make the approach to force as gradual as possible, bring the pressure on very slowly.

I use the same methods to get a dog started lining in the water. Bird boys can be hidden out of sight. You take the dog out and set him up, give him the build-up—"mark, mark"—and about that time, when the bird boy hears me say "mark" the second time, he throws out a bird. The first time, maybe he can shoot and throw; the second time, he can throw the bird without shooting. Then the next time, if the dog is going cheerfully, the bird is already out, and he thinks that he just missed seeing it thrown. Or I let him watch a bird thrown, put him back, wait a while, and then send him.

Perhaps the big thing in building up enthusiasm, along with time and work, is being a little more enthusiastic ourselves.

Stopping on the Whistle

I teach a dog to sit to the whistle first in the yard, as a puppy; I tap his rump with the whip as I blow a short blast. Then, if it ever becomes necessary to stop him with a BB, slingshot, or bird shot, maybe that tap on the rump will mean something to him.

Later, I start a young dog stopping and sitting to the whistle a few feet from me. I do this first with the dog coming at me. I leave the dog sitting, back away from him, whistle him to me, and when he is about three or four feet from me, blow the whistle to stop. I use a threat, a gesture with the whip toward the dog. If need be, I put a long check cord on the dog and throw it around a post or wire behind him, so that I can stop the dog with the cord as he is coming toward me when I blow the whistle. Most dogs want to come all the way in to heel before they sit, so it is important to get the idea over to them to sit right where they are. Run out, sit the dog, and then move back to where you were.

When a dog is stopping well under these conditions, that is, when he really knows what that blast on the whistle means, then I teach him to stop out in the field. I know that I am probably going to have a problem the first time, so I anticipate it and set up the training session to be prepared for it. After I send the dog on a line, I start edging out to be in a good position to reach him when I blow that whistle. As I get older and slower, I try to get farther out to be in a better relative position to get out there fast and get to the dog. A younger fellow can work farther away. But when I hit the dog with that whistle, I want to be close enough so that I can stop him. If the dog stops, fine and dandy, but if not, I am on the dead run. If a dog senses, when he hears that whistle, that you are coming, I think he is apt to stop and turn around and look with expectancy. That expectancy is probably as important as anything in getting him to stop.

Sometimes, to punish a dog for not stopping in the field, especially if you are unable to run out each time to reach the dog, it is helpful to make him sit for awhile before casting him. It is a meditation period. It can be almost as effective, though maybe not as quick, as a more severe form of correction. With a tougher dog, one that is bull-headed, you can give him a violent shaking and sitting down, accompanied with the whistle. Make it an impressive lesson, so that there won't have to be too many repeats. Try not to get two or three refusals before you get to the dog. Just one blast, and that's all—you're on the run out to get him. To give more encourages disobedience.

Handling On A Mark   The day will come when you will have to stop your dog and handle him on the way to a mark. This is one of those times when you must know your dog. It may be a good lesson which will teach him something he'll never forget, but if it is timed badly it may take him weeks to recover from it. If you decide that the time has come, then quit pulling your punches.

Set up a test with a dead bird thrown to the left and a live bird, which will run, thrown straight ahead on the other side of a strong, preferably woven wire fence, which the dog cannot get through but can see through. Seeing it run, he will go for the live bird. Then give him the whistle about halfway to the fence, and when he does not stop, sting him with bird shot. It is a severe lesson, and you hope the end results warrant it. He can't possibly get the live bird through the fence, no danger of that. When you have stopped him, give him a left cast to the dead bird in as mild and gentle a manner as you can, as if nothing had happened.

Sometimes one tough lesson is better and less brutal than weeks of nagging. Bird shot is less disturbing to some dogs than a whip or loud words. Every dog accepts each form of punishment differently. Some soldiers fear the bayonet, some bullets, some bombs, some artillery, all with a different degree of fear. Sometimes, if persisted in, some fears will make a soldier a mental case. By the same token, some forms of punishment can make a dog bug-eyed and practically bring on a nervous breakdown. Maybe it's a folded newspaper that scares the hell out of him.

I knew a man who was chided by his wife for inhumane treatment when using bird shot on his dog. "Honey," he said, "it doesn't hurt," and he handed her the gun. He measured off the right distance, bent over, and told her to fire. She did. Unfortunately, he forgot that he had on light slacks instead of heavy duck pants, and maybe he was a foot or two short in his distance. He spent a painful week. So if you do this, be sure of the size shot you use, and be sure of the distance. Better get expert assistance. Plan the lesson well, so that you don't need to repeat it. After one lesson like this, just a shot in the air will suffice to remind the dog, as a rule.

Freezing on the Whistle

When a dog freezes on the whistle, that is, when he just sits and refuses to move, refuses to take a cast, I have found a threat of the whip will sometimes loosen him from his freeze. This problem is often brought on by an intense feeling of confusion, and the habit can be a bad one. This type of dog sits and sits on a whistle stop while you are trying frantically to cast him. He looks at you with all the innocence of a schoolboy, and seems to be saying, "I am confused; I don't know what you want; and besides, your antics are so funny, I will just sit and watch you."

A quick start towards him and a threatening gesture of the whip with an underhand swipe will sometimes get the dog off his fanny as if he had sat on a bumblebee. To get the full potential, he must at one time have had the experience of tasting the whip in an all-out effort. Don't use it naggingly, but when you have to use it, make it impressive. A gesture will, thereafter, have added significance. Go all the way with it only occasionally.

If you anticipate this problem with a dog in a trial, and if it is the over cast that he is inclined to freeze on, try giving the come whistle, or a back cast. Freezing is almost the same reaction that causes a point—fixation by intensity, a hypnotic state. Sometimes a quick cast before the dog has slipped fully into the state will suffice; or you can even start to walk in the direction of the over cast before giving it. If you have used a prod in training, sometimes a threatening advance while waving the prod will unseat a dog.

Freezing, or the tendency to freeze, cannot be cured all at once. The big thing, when sensing its approach, is to stop its full development by acting fast and preventing the habit from forming.

Running a pattern can also help to prevent it. The dog is put in a groove; he goes where he has gone many times; in fact, he almost anticipates the next move. Pattern running can, in this case, be a wonderful corrective measure. But sometimes, if patterns are persisted in too much, they can cause such trouble. Frequent shifts are advisable to fresh ground, different scenery and terrain, a different view. But at other times, it is best to get back to the old groove and put the dog back in his familiar chute. Confidence is the most important factor in curing a dog from freezing on the whistle.

Some trainers don't believe in pattern training. They always want fresh ground, different ground, different tests. I believe that if used in moderation, pattern training can accomplish wonders with a minimum of time and effort. But no doubt, it can be overdone.

Patterns can be used for exercise early in the morning. When the dog is first let out and is chock-full of fire and energy, let him run it off in the pattern. Certainly it helps the dogs at the start on blinds; it makes their blinds into semi-blinds, and the transition from hot marks to cold blinds is not so abrupt for them. It's great for certain types of dogs. A top trainer soon senses if he has that type of dog, one for whom pattern running will do miracles. Know your dog; know the type of training he accepts best, and the type of punishment he accepts best, from mild to harsh. Always know how far you can go. And to keep that tail up and happy, always end up with a little fun. Keep the dog in good spirits.

Forcing in the Water

I think your greatest concern in having a good water dog, or to keep from ruining one who could be a good water dog, is to keep the dog happy, to keep the water a pleasant picture. If all the dog sees when he is around the water is the whip, prod, rope, and shotgun, or if every time he comes to the water he is yanked in, ducked, and half drowned, all you are doing in reality is converting the water hole into a Chamber of Horrors.

Let the dog have shore-line retrieves and retrieves back up on land. Get in the water and have the dog retrieve on land, and then deliver to hand in the water. Make it all just another retrieve, no worse than any other. Don't build up a complex about the water. Start the lesson with fun and end up with fun.

But in every dog's life, there comes a time when he refuses the water. He quits when it ceases to be fun. This is very likely to happen when the pressure is applied on his cold water blinds. Your approach must be careful but firm. Forcing in the water must be done as gently as possible, and with as little intimidation as possible.

I have seen it done with rope and boat, and much yelling, shouting, and beating hell out of the dog, one man whipping and one man yanking. Sometimes it leaves a dog bug-eyed. It leaves a picture of the water the dog will never forget, and it can make him a nervous wreck.

In the summer, put on your shorts and tennis shoes, and put the dog on a short leash. Hold the leash with your left hand, and pull the dog into the water as you wade in with him; with your right hand, gesture with a whip over his rump. You may not even have to hit him. He can sense the arm and the movement. Do it mildly and quietly, but as firmly as possible. I have felt that dogs are usually treated too harshly at this stage, and that the picture is always bad. Sometimes it can never be erased.

For many dogs this mild forcing may be all that is needed, but for others a somewhat sterner method may be necessary. Send your helper out in a boat about 25 or 30 yards from shore, or place him across a body of water about that wide. Experienced help is essential here, and you'd do best to have an experienced trainer assisting you, for this can be a dangerous maneuver. A long plastic rope is attached to the dog's collar, and the other end is held by the helper in the boat. Put your left hand on this rope and, as you give the command to send the dog, you pull the dog toward the water with your left hand. The helper in the boat should pull, too. At the same time, as the dog leaves, give him a little switch across the rump with a whip in your right hand. If need be, make the first switch a trifle hard, so that he feels it. The helper continues to pull, gathering up the rope so that the dog does not get tangled in it. Once again, be as quiet and mild as possible. Let there be no unnecessary noise or punishment.

Repeat this until the dog goes of his own accord when sent. At first, you can throw a dummy out in the water after the dog has started, or have the helper throw it. After the dog does this well, eliminate the helper and the boat and use a short leash; jerk it with your left hand and fan the dog's rear with the whip in your right hand. You might even have to start in with him. I would do this until he will enter the water to retrieve several times in a row, going at the command for a dummy that he did not see being thrown.

Then end up with fun retrieves; try to brighten the picture without making a complete apology for what you are teaching the dog. You are not asking forgiveness for what you are making the dog do—you are just trying to give him some association with the water that is pleasant rather than horrible.

I have had dogs brought to me who folded up at the sight of water and wanted to run away. And these were dogs who had liked the water. It was a man-made fault, as most faults are. I walked with these dogs on leash around the shore quietly. Then I'd take bread smeared with bacon grease, which the dogs love. With a dog on leash, I would first give some to him by throwing pieces along the shore, or even back on land. I wanted him to learn he was not going to get beaten into the water every time he saw it; I wanted to suggest a normal time, a happy time, and to erase the horrible picture that he had in his mind. Then I'd throw the bread at the water's edge. Another time, I'd walk into the water with the dog at heel and throw the bread up on land, gently pulling the dog back to me with the leash when he'd eaten it, rewarding him with more bread each time he came to me. I did this until his miserable picture became a pleasant one, and then I'd start back on a normal training schedule, from the beginning.

I had a dog, Buccaneer Pat, who would not go in the water. He would not leave your side to go in the water. He was a mature dog, and as a puppy he had been a good water dog, had never refused it. But now his owner and trainer had given up. Yet in two weeks I was able to win a sanctioned trial with him, and all the tests were water tests.

At that time I had a wild bunch of unrestrained dogs who were chained up near the spot where we were working, waiting their turn to work in the water. They were a noisy, motley bunch, always fighting and tugging to get loose. I chained Pat here, and a more dejected creature I have never seen. He acted like he was trying to grind himself into the ground. But at the end of the day, he was peeking out of the corner of his eye. On the second day he was watching, and on the third day, when I was about halfway through, he got so excited that he let out a yip. Then I ran back to him, took him to the line, gave him a shot duck, and sent him quick. I followed this procedure until he became one of Morgan's unruly dogs, tugging and straining to get loose. He took his turn, worked in the orthodox way, and was quite happy about it. I was careful not to make the tests too hard.

That weekend, the people at the trial nudged each other when he came to the line, informing their less trial-wise friends that, "this dog won't go in the water." Lo and behold, we had a water blind. I thought I was surely sunk, but I tried to act natural and send him off with the same actions, the same confidence and build-up, that I had used in the previous two weeks. I guess in my excitement I momentarily forgot that he might fail; and he forgot it too, because the gallery of experts was dumbfounded when he tore into the water.

When forcing dogs in the water, it must not be done half-way. It is the most delicate situation in training a retriever, if you expect him to go all the way in trials. The dog is not always going to be happy. He is going to be sour at times, dejected; he'll go out slowly, just miserably, and pussy-foot into the water with his head and ears down and his rump floating high. He'll look back, and all you'll see are the whites of his eyes.

In your mind, you have become an object of ridicule to your friends, so you decide to call it all off before the lesson is thoroughly learned, and sweeten the dog up to make him look good. He bounces back and forgives you. Soon, he is plunging into the water on the break, everybody is happy, and all is forgiven. And the lesson, incidentally, is thrown down the drain.

Regardless of how bad the dog looks at first, if he keeps on going— even if he hesitates, but keeps on going of his own accord—you have it made, brother, and all your struggles were worth it; the rest of the way is just a question of time and patience. Some dogs snap out of it faster than others; usually it is a matter of months, but sometimes it may be next year. You hear the statement, "Old Joe is beginning to jell," and your work is now paying off. The fact of it is, the dog is forgetting all the unpleasantness, all the drudgery and misery. But you don't want him to forget it all, even if he shows a touch of reluctance. For a well-trained dog will prove himself under all conditions and all circumstances; he'll keep going with absolutely no water refusals, regardless of the weather. You don't want him to be too miserable, but you do want him to be beyond the state of questioning the order. The dog becomes happier in time, but never expect, or want, a complete state of forgiveness.

It is this then: the water determines the trial; all the spirit must not be taken out of the dog; but neither should all the spirit be left in.

Advanced Lines

To win today, a dog's line must be good; line work is all-important. When a judge lays out a blind with obstacles or hazards along the way, you don't have to ask him how he wants it done; and the quicker you have to fight your dog to keep on that line, the more severe the penalty.

Remember your beginning drills, where dummies are put out in a pile, and the handler keeps moving back and changing his position to make the lines longer and more difficult, but always sending the dog to the same spot each time. Dr. Evans made a great line dog out of Gilmore's Peggy by throwing dummies out of the car in series, 15 yards apart, and driving on for 50 yards before stopping and sending Peggy back, increasing the distance with each workout. When a dog is lining well under these conditions, when he knows his pattern drills well and is stopping and casting, then it is time to start on the more advanced lines by diversions, through obstacles, with hard angles into the water, etc.

Diversion Marks When I first start a young dog on blinds in conjunction with diversion marks, I like to go back to the area where he has had his patterns, where he knows his pattern blinds by heart. First, he'll run his pattern blind. Then maybe give him a shot bird off to the right, almost at right-angles to the line to the blind. Let him pick the bird up, and then turn and run the pattern blind again. Next time, maybe give him a shot bird, but make him take the blind first. He has done this blind hundreds of times, he knows a bird is out there, so he should do it in the face of a marked bird at right angles. Another time, I might have two marked birds, one on each side, and then run the pattern blind between them.

When you are teaching a dog to run a blind alongside cover or woods where he has just had a mark, start with a mark out of the cover in the spot you want to put the blind. Then you can give a mark in the cover, and then back to the original mark, to a bird the dog did not see put out. It's a semi-blind really, but it gets the dog started without destroying his confidence. It will help you avoid having to go out and punish the dog, avoid having to be tough with the dog. That's the secret of good training, isn't it? To do it with as little punishment as possible, but as firmly as possible and as gradually as possible, and to give the dog the advantage of every doubt. I don't say we could compete in our trials without a whip, but the basic training can be done without a whip by showing the dog what you want. It is after he is trained to do it thoroughly, and won't, that the whip comes in.

Later on, you can run this same drill and get the blind before the mark. He has run the blind enough times to know it is there, so shoot a bird in the cover and make him pick up the blind out of the cover first. It is a good drill in handling, a good drill in taking a line, so occasionally reverse your order and pick up the blind first. In training, for an experienced dog, it is a good idea to make him pick up the blind first, but don't do it too often.

It is also good training, with experienced dogs, to reverse the order occasionally on marks, and make the dog take the first bird thrown first and the last bird last. It is a good drill in taking your line, but be careful not to do it too much—you would like a dog to be able to do it when necessary.

When you go back to the area where the dog is familiar with his pattern blinds, it breaks him into the problem of diversions more easily. The dog looks out and he knows there is a bird out there. He goes with confidence, and it is easier to turn him away from diversion marks and make him run the blinds he knows.

Apart from the patterns, be careful about returning an experienced dog to the same blind on a test again and again to get perfection on his line. It is better to settle for a little imperfection than to develop the habit of always returning to the same place, or else it may be difficult later to get the dog to take a fine angle away from a line he has previously taken, or a line close by a mark.

Through Cover   A dog should learn to take a line through cover without a path; he should be willing to make his own path, holding the line you give him. Start up close to a hedgerow or a row of high grass, and teach him to go straight through into open ground for a dummy or a bird that he can see when he gets out there. The same type of drill is helpful in teaching a dog to go through heavy cover and out into open water.

If you can get a dog to go through a wall, why, you almost have it made on your lines. But if your dog is going to look for a path, and if the path isn't a good path, you're going to be in trouble. In a trial, you will do everything you can to move over two or three feet to avoid it. But in training, you are going to teach your dog not to take the obvious path

FC Chevrier's Golden Rod, owned by Mr. C. N. Batts, delivers a bird to Charley Morgan, October 28, 1950. *Photograph: Evelyn M. Shafer.*

Coffee of Bohland Hill, owned by Mr. P. Webster, and Charley Morgan. Klamath Falls, Oregon, 1949. *Photograph: James C. Moreland.*

Charley Morgan takes a bird from FC Nelgard's King Tut, March 19, 1948, Big Meadow Farm, Deer Island, Oregon. *Photograph: James C. Moreland.*

Labrador Retriever Club, East Islip, L.I., New York, October 27–28, 1945. FC Firelei of Deer Creek, owned by Mrs. H. E. Le-Gear, delivers a pheasant to Charley Morgan. *Photograph: Percy T. Jones.*

FC Gilmore's Peggy, owned by Dr. L. M. Evans, delivering to Charley Morgan. Deer Island, Oregon, March, 1948. *Photograph: James C. Moreland.*

FC Chevrier's Golden Rod, owned by Mr. C. N. Batts, takes off to retrieve. Klamath Falls, Oregon, 1949. *Photograph: James C. Moreland.*

Klamath Falls, Oregon, 1949. FC Nelgard's King Tut, owned by Mt. Joy Kennels, with his handler, Charley Morgan. *Photograph: James C. Moreland.*

unless he is sent that way, but to make his own path when taking the line you give him.

Start out close to the cover, obstacle, wall, or whatever you are trying to send the dog through. When the dog has learned to hold a line through it, gradually back farther and farther away each time you send him. I start close and move back on lines across obstacles, over ditches, down gulleys, angling across roads or corn rows. If the dog fails, I shorten the test, ease up on it, get closer to the obstacle, trying to avoid as much pressure and punishment as possible.

But I do think that when a dog is refusing and refusing, just not doing what you tell him to do, and you are sure that he is clear in his mind about what is expected of him, then I think he should be punished. Then I call him back and scold him with tongue and whip. Generally the whip is better. If you are a folded-newspaper addict, use the newspaper—but never the *Toledo Blade*; that is too severe.

I think a little round clump of weeds, a pothole, or a blind wall of grass along the side of a road where there is no path, can teach a dog that there is just one thing to do, and that is to take your line and keep on it. As he progresses, I make the line longer and longer.

John Olin once asked me, "What makes a dog take a line?" And I answered, "Did you ever see a dog chasing a jack rabbit? When the dog about catches the rabbit, the rabbit lays back his ears, and that is when he really takes a line." I think that a little fear is in him, and he is going; I think that is a good explanation of a line. Maybe, at first, you have to make a dog run "from" and not "to." He'll be running "from" that which he fears, but then he'll get into gear and run "to" the bird to be retrieved.

Once, in St. Louis, when my dog Rosie (Cream City Co-ed) was just out of the Derby and running in the Open, she looked awfully piggy on a blind; she was reluctant, hesitant, and just looked bad, but she kept going. D. L. said, "Chuck, you have got her; she kept going." And she did. Sometimes it is a slow, drawn-out affair, but as soon as the dog keeps going, bad as he may look, lay off the pressure. You don't want him to look too bad; you'd rather have some degree of happiness; but really, the dog who goes out with moderate speed is possibly a more dependable line dog over obstacles, off points, and through ditches and fences. This dog is reflecting; he is going because he is told to; he is not just taking a run. If you can get him to do it happily but with a certain degree of responsibility —brother, you have made it. I will take the dog who runs because he is told to rather than the one who runs from sheer delight.

Angles Into The Water   When I start dogs on angles into the water, I look for places that have an artificial barrier, something that the dog cannot run around, so that he is forced to cut into the water. Possibly it's a boat, or it may be a hill, a stump, or a fence. All these can be used to help a dog take an angle into the water, and you should take advantage of places like that.

Or use paths that angle into the water at the start. Once a fellow saw me giving a crunchon to a dog who was reluctant to return to me in training, and he said, "You can't do that in a trial." Sure you can't. But you can get the dog started, and all these artificial things help at the start. We use them at first to get the dog doing the right thing, and then we'll get away from them later on.

So if you can find a path that angles into the water, start the dog on it, close to the water's edge, and then keep moving back until you can send him 50 to 75 yards back from the shore, and he'll still hold the line; send him on blind retrieves for big white plastic dummies that he can see, dummies that float high.

I get the dog to go as far as I think he will on his own, and then I have the duck out 100 yards farther, so well-trained that, at my cue, he will flap his wings. "What a break!" I do this by not using a duck at all—the unpredictable SOBs. I settle for a large floating white or yellow dummy that can be seen 100 yards away. In other words, when my dogs go on a water blind, they go with the expectation of keeping on going for 200 yards, or until they run into something, or hear the whistle. They know darn well that their dummy is on that path. Ninety percent of the time it is directly on that path; and 10 percent of the time, it will call for a right or left hand cast at the 200-yard point.

After your dog gets going pretty well, try to avoid using paths too much; work him through rushes or grass, where he can't see what is on the other side. You had better check the cover first for rocks or holes. Never let your dog run the bank; you will want him to learn to take lines from straight into the water, to fine angles almost parallel to the shore. You can do pattern training up to a certain point, and you can always fall back on it for confidence in the old familiar spots and paths where the dog learned his lines originally.

When a dog fails on the angle into the water, when he does not take the angle you give him but wants to go either straight in or run down the shore line, you can call him back, punish him, and start over from the same spot, or you can shorten the distance to the shore. My method is to shorten

the distance and make the test easier. I feel that a dog has only so many
lickings coming, and if you reach the saturation point, you have no dog.

You hear people say, "Never give a shore-line retrieve." Sure, give
the dogs shore-line retrieves, but back far enough from the edge so that
it is definite, and then give a retrieve in the water. If a dog fails he is
punished for not taking the line, not for refusing the water. It becomes bad
psychology to punish the dog constantly for refusing the water. The idea
gets over to the dog that he must get into that water, and then fine lines
just off shore become impossible. The dog wants to get in at once, and in
his desire to get in it is hard to keep him from going straight in—he just
won't take that fine angle. Judges set up tests that demand fine angles for
this very purpose, to see if your dog will take that line.

I think an occasional shore-line retrieve for an advanced dog—a
retrieve back on shore, and then one in the water—is a good idea. Turn
away from the water and give retrieves back on land, so that the dog
doesn't always think that the minute he sees water, he is going to be
forced into it. A dog can and does get too much over a long period of time
around the water, until only one thought remains: "Get in that water or
you are going to have hell beaten out of you." Punish a dog for the line,
not the water—get that idea over to him.

It's difficult to get the water entry at an angle to be a happy and
dependable one; it is a "must" job and not a request. Your dog can be
depended upon best if he is just a little down, but always end up your water
sessions with play, with the old breaking razzle-dazzle.

In training, my water blinds are always in the water, by points, beyond
islands, and across dikes; never on land, never in the rushes, but always
beyond them. You want the dog to know that he must always keep going
and looking. It's harder to get a dog to look, to search with his eyes, than
it is to get him to use his nose. Don't ever let a dog get into the habit of
landing, or into the habit of hunting the rushes. Fight him off the land to
the point where he won't refuse the land completely, but would rather not
go there because he doesn't expect to find his bird there. Get him to the
point where it takes a command and a cast to land him, but he can be landed.

The same is also true for islands or points. It does not take much to
get a dog land-minded, point-minded, island-minded. When in doubt, he
must be obsessed with one idea—to keep going, to keep looking beyond.
Your big white floating dummies are a help here. Get a dog out as far as
he will go on his own, and then put the blind about 75 yards farther out
in the water, where he can see it. I think the floating blind is the greatest

training blind in the world. Normally I never put a water blind on land. Unless you run into a problem, it is a simple matter in a trial to cast most dogs up on land. That is one of the big secrets of good training in the water—always put the blind in the water and, above all, not in the rushes.

To control a dog who is fairly well advanced, one who should know how to take an angle into the water without running down the bank, I like to put a long plastic rope on his collar and hold on to the end of it. If he takes the line, I let go and just let him drag it; but the second he starts veering down at the water's edge, I yank him back. Sometimes I punish him where he started to veer off his line, where he made his mistake. If that doesn't work, then I try taking him back and punishing him again where I started him. I say, "Get back," and punish him with the whip. Sometimes this works and sometimes it doesn't, but you have got to keep that dog under control. Just as soon as he varies from what he was told to do, just as soon as the mistake starts, almost at the moment it enters his mind, you can control him. But some dogs are almost impossible to teach to angle into the water.

This will work with soft dogs, perhaps better than the harsher methods. The dog can be controlled and corrected without severe punishment. Always remember to do everything you can to keep the water from being a bad picture. Start with fun and end with fun.

Before you punish a dog for not taking or holding a line, whether on land or in the water, you must be absolutely sure in your own mind that the dog knows what he should do and what he is being punished for. I like to give a dog the benefit of the doubt. When a dog makes a mistake, I don't punish him at all at first; I bring him clear back, scold him, and send him again. I give him a chance to correct himself of his own accord by drilling and repetition. It is only after he persists, when I know that he knows he is doing wrong, that I get after him severely with the whip, or possibly even the prod, depending on what type of punishment is best for that dog. I think I have tried every method on some dog or other over the years.

When a dog lands and comes up on shore, leaves the water on a water blind, I use the bird shot. If he has refused my cast and deliberately climbed on to a point or island, I try to hit him just as he is getting out of the water.

It is also possible to correct him by having your helper out there with a prod; that can scare the life out of a dog. Now with certain types of dogs, maybe that is what you want; it may be necessary. But I have seen dogs who became hard or almost impossible to land after a session like that. Good training is balanced training; you try not to overdo or underdo any part of it. If you can keep a dog from going to the point, if his tendency is not to land but to keep going, yet you can always land him if you want to, then you have a well-trained dog.

By the same token, if you call a dog back too often to correct him for not taking a line, you may run into problems with recasts. Yet if you use bird shot or a slingshot to correct a dog by stinging him as he is veering off his line, you may start the dog popping. So try to vary your corrections; keep your training diversified and balanced, and always keep the individual dog in mind, and the type of correction that he takes best.

I have tried using an electric collar, and I have watched others use it, but I don't care much for that method. Maybe in certain cases the electric collar can accomplish a great deal—if you wanted to teach a dog to keep away from a road, perhaps, or off a point, he might possibly associate the shock with that area. But I do think that the electric collar can be very dangerous, and it is debatable in my mind whether it hurts a dog more than it helps him.

Advanced Casts

How well your dog casts will depend a lot on your early pattern training. Remember to make the casts in your patterns long, so that the dog won't get into the habit of short, hacking casts. If he has a tendency to angle back on his over casts, you can try to overcome this by bringing the right and left dummies a little closer toward you in your patterns. Send the dog out on the center line, stop him at the stopping point, and give him a right over. The right dummies should be closer in, so that the dog will have to angle in somewhat on his over cast. The same should be done on the left. This will help to keep him from swinging back on his overs if he has developed that tendency.

Some dogs get into the bad habit of scalloping back on an over, not really taking an over cast at all but going directly back. If the dog has been well schooled, well drilled in his patterns, and knows he should take a proper over but is deliberately scalloping back, then you had best set up a trap and sting him. Send him out, stop him, give him the over, and when he digs back, sting him in the rear with .22 bird shot, or with the shotgun if the distance is great enough. You must get him instantly; by the time you can run out there with a folded newspaper, the effect will be lost. After you have stung him, bring him back to the stopping point and give him the same over cast. When he takes it, praise him, and then try the other over. You may never need to repeat this lesson; if the dog starts slipping back on his overs again, just the sound of the gun should remind him. But before you do this, be absolutely sure that he knows his casts thoroughly.

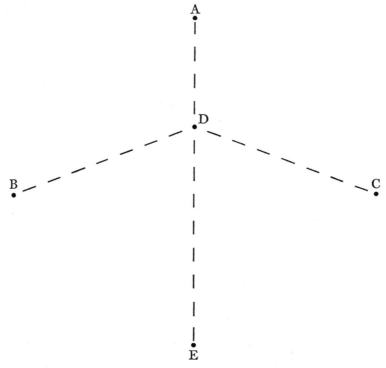

Pattern to correct dog who is angling back on his over casts. Dummies at B and C should force dog to angle in from his stopping point at D.

Casts into the wind can often cause a dog to scallop. Some dogs have a natural dread of going into the wind, and it's almost impossible to get them over this. Try to work them on marked birds into the wind more often. Give them more drills, more patterns with lines and casts into the wind. Don't work your dogs down wind all the time.

Sometimes we pivot right or left on a back cast, but is it a good idea to manipulate a quarter cast? If persisted in, your casts will never be accurate. There should be just four casts: left and right over, back, and come in. In your training, try to make these casts as accurate as possible. Know your dog's strengths and weaknesses; some dogs cast better in one direction than another, so drill according to your dog's weaknesses. Generally, back casts should be given more than side casts. Never fail to drill a dog on the come whistle frequently. It is difficult to get a dog to come in if he is a good hunting dog. Control on the come in whistle is the most difficult form of control.

In a trial, try to maneuver your dog to use his strength in handling. If he is weak on a certain cast, try to avoid getting in a position where you will have to use that cast. Also, remember to use the commands "over" and "back" rather than "get over" or "get back." Dogs are quick to start on the "get" without waiting for the rest of the command; the fewer words you use the better.

For long casts in the water, I like to have a hidden bird boy throw a dummy at the same time that I give the dog a cast. If I have sent the dog out 100 yards on a line in the water, I blow the whistle; when the dog stops and turns, I give him a right cast and the boy throws a big white dummy 100 yards to the right. The dog will see it—or the splash—and 100 yards is a good cast in anyone's book.

The same method is good in training for channel blinds. If I am having trouble keeping a dog straight up the middle, I have a bird boy heave out a dummy into the middle, maybe 100 yards down the channel. Try doing this occasionally into the wind; send your dog up a channel into the wind, and after you have blown the whistle and given a back cast up the channel into the wind—a cast the dog really will not want to take—have a dummy thrown.

It is a good idea to train for certain casts by walking your dog out, sitting and leaving him, walking back, and giving him the cast. You will get the benefit of cast training without continually lining your dog out and stopping him, lining and stopping—a routine that can sometimes start a dog popping.

A good example of this is training for a cast off the shore into the water. Sometimes in a trial you have a situation where a dog has to go down the shore line for a distance and then take a cast into the water. You don't want to train your dog to run down the shore line, so it is a good idea, in training, to leave him on the shore, walk back, and give him the cast into the water. This is an important cast for him to know; a dog has got to learn to take a cast into the water from a distance. In a trial, a dog can occasionally slide off a little on a fine angle into the water. He may start to run the bank, and maybe one whistle and cast into the water won't get you thrown out. A dog can sometimes panic in this situation; he knows he is in trouble; but if you have trained him on this cast, you can come out all right.

In the old days, we used to have tests like this much more often, and we would train for them more. I had the yellow Lab, Ben (Chevrier's Golden Rod), and I would send him down the bank and try to cast him in the water, and it was almost impossible if he was back a little from the edge. So I hid a fellow behind a tree, and after I gave Ben the cast, the man stung him with a marble. Pretty soon, Ben would take a cast into the water from 50 yards back. Ben didn't really like the water—he was man-made entirely, as far as the water was concerned—but Mr. Batts of Santa Fe said that Ben was the finest water dog he had ever had; he just never thought of him refusing the water.

Whether a dog likes or dislikes the water doesn't necessarily have a lot to do with how good a water dog he becomes, especially as far as blind retrieves in the water are concerned. The more they like the water, the better; but usually, to be reliable, they end up by having to be forced every inch. But you would like to have them go in as happily as possible.

Advanced Stopping

When you have trouble stopping a dog on the whistle at a distance, or in difficult situations such as at the edge of high cover, there are several methods of correction you can try. On land, you can try getting out after the dog yourself. The minute he refuses a whistle, you are on the run after him. Get him as fast as you can, and make the lesson effective. Blow a blast on the whistle as you use the whip: "peep," "sit," and crack the whip across his rump. Then leave him sitting there to meditate while you go back to your original spot to handle him.

Immediate punishment is essential. So if you are anticipating trouble, move out to be in a position to grab the dog as fast as possible. An older person, or someone who doesn't care to break any track records, had better have his dog more thoroughly trained before getting into this situation.

But regardless of how well trained the dog is in the beginning, there comes a time when he has to be reached and corrected instantly or you have lost a lot of ground. By the time you are able to get out there, if it is a considerable distance, the dog has gone into the cover and has had a fine time hunting. Before you can grab him and drag him back to the spot where he refused the whistle, he has undoubtedly forgotten what the punishment is for because there has been too much delay. After he has been on his own for a while hunting the cover, he just doesn't know what it is that he is getting punished for.

So there comes a point when a refusal of the whistle at a distance must be followed by some immediate punishment. Stinging the dog with no. 8s from the shotgun at a proper distance is probably most effective. It should be done by an experienced trainer, and there is an element of danger in it. But once the dog has been stung, just a shot in the air will be enough the next time—better really, since it doesn't panic him. A good trainer certainly doesn't shoot at a dog every time he uses the gun in training.

The assistance of a helper is needed when you are teaching a dog to stop in the water off points or close to the bank in channels. The helper can use a prod or whip. Sometimes a light bamboo fish pole six or eight feet long is effective in reaching a dog out in the water; an old-fashioned buggy whip is also excellent for making threatening gestures at a dog to keep him in the water. If the dog refuses your whistle and heads for the land, the helper, who has been hidden, comes out after him. For some dogs, just the surprise of finding someone there is sufficient to drive them back into the water.

Of course, the helper must act on the advice of the trainer: "Go carefully with this dog; use the whip sparingly; even a gesture will do"; or "go all out with this SOB; use the prod; and don't let him bull his way to land." Between these two extremes, every dog is handled differently. With one dog, you don't dare use a slingshot; for another one, hide the prod; and for this unruly, bull-headed SOB, you've got to get real rough. You must instruct your helper what to use and how far to go on every dog. "On this dog, keep out of sight. I will handle him myself, and will sting him with bird shot if he lands. I am convinced that is the way to handle this dog." If you use bird shot in the water, use it very carefully; be sure that the dog is at a safe distance and is turned away from you. If a dog refuses the whistle at a distance in open water, you can get in a boat and get out there after him.

So every dog requires a different instrument of discipline applied with a different degree of severity. These are things that the head trainer decides. It is thought out carefully before each test; the test is laid out in anticipation of correcting certain faults; the dog is really invited to do something wrong; and you tell the helper what to do and how far to go.

One important thing: yelling and shouting is out. There should be no panicky scenes. Everything is done as quietly as possible; never raise your voice unless absolutely necessary; learn to control your dogs with a minimum of effort and noise. You can't shout at a dog on the line at a trial, and if you can control him without bothering the other dogs and handlers, or the incoming ducks in the duck blind, you are all right. A continually noisy handler disturbs the other dogs and handlers, and perhaps causes incoming ducks to flare away from the blind. He should be dealt with severely.

Channel Blinds

Whether we approve of a channel blind or not, we had better not neglect it in the training of our dogs if we are going to win any trials. At one time a channel blind was quite popular, but it has now been recognized to be a poor hunting test. However, along about the last or next-to-last series, when the judges are having trouble coming up with a winner, this test, or a corrupt form of it, is often resorted to; it is the court of last resort. In preparing your dog to win, don't overlook it. It may be no good as a hunting test, but the field trial judges still find it useful to separate the men from the boys.

Some dogs master it easily—they seem to have a natural love of cruising up and down a channel. But with the average dog, from his first introduction to the water, it has been a battle to drive him out from the shore. And his training has been to go across; going down the channel is something different, something unusual. Up to now, you have always been fighting to get him across.

When you start having trouble, a dog quickly grasps this from your voice or from the tone of your whistle. He knows immediately that you are getting excited, or worse, annoyed. You are letting the dog know that a desperate situation is arising. At a trial you don't yell, "get back, you no-good SOB," but your whistle quickly carries that message, and the battle is on. All the struggles of the dog's early youth come back to him, and he starts fighting you, going from one shore to the other.

To do a channel blind well you must be calm and confident, and you must keep your dog that way. So the most important thing is to build up the dog's confidence and try to overcome his fear of working in the water. So put on your shorts and tennis shoes and prepare for the basic lesson.

Wade out into the channel yourself, into the middle if it is shallow enough, and give the dog a little heeling, sitting and staying practice in the channel. Reward his "come" with a tidbit. This relaxes a dog and gives him confidence in you in a strange place, a strange set-up. He gets the feel of the bottom in the channel, and this helps to overcome his fear.

After you have done this, you can start him on short retrieves up and down the channel. Make them short, quick retrieves until all signs of fear or nervousness leave him. When he is settled and has regained his poise, get him wild with excitement to help restore his full eagerness. Make it all fun. Use the old razzle-dazzle. Let him—even encourage him—to break, giving him his "fun cue" by waving the dummy around your head and saying "okay," or "let's go." Give the dog the recess bell so that the break will not interfere with his staunching.

Then go to the second stage: walk down the channel with him, dropping the dummies as you go. Use the white, high-floating plastic dummies, and drop them at intervals of about 15 yards. After you have dropped about three or four, and the dog has seen you do it, go on about 50 yards farther. Then turn and give him the command to retrieve. The dummies should be easily visible. Keep retiring down the channel, so that by the time the last dummy is retrieved, it is at least 100 yards away.

You should have two well-schooled helpers with you now to keep the dog from going to shore on his return. It is very important that the dog is never allowed to return by land. If he did, it would undo all the good of making him go by the middle of the channel. Your helpers should be well trained and experienced. Go over the problems of each dog with them to decide how far you and they can go in fighting that dog off the shore. Decide what instruments should be used, whip, prod, or fish pole—whichever is best for each individual dog. For a timid, soft dog, a threatening gesture is sufficient.

The exact procedure for each dog must be decided upon. Don't let your helpers go too far; harsh methods can do a lot of harm. But the lesson should be severe enough so that you will be a little alarmed for fear you might have gone too far. You don't want the dog to forget it quickly. Yet, you don't want it to be so severe that the dog is obsessed with just one idea: to stay in the channel. He could get so that he can't be landed on a point or put across an island. If he is just a little reluctant to land, then you have got him.

Try letting the dog drag a plastic rope during this stage of his training. You started him on it when he was first learning to line into the water, and at his first mistake you can drag him back, punish him, and recast him. He will get the idea that the best thing to do is to stay in the middle and keep going. He has the feeling that you are controlling him. Even a short leash for him to drag gives you some extra control.

When the dog will swim down the channel about 100 yards before he

starts looking around, station a bird boy about 75 or 100 yards farther on
and have him throw out a dummy into the middle of the channel at a pre-
arranged signal which you give when you think that the dog has reached
his limit. Then send the dog back the full distance with the dummy already
out. Eventually, the dog should be able to swim the length of the channel
for the visible white floating dummy—200 yards or more. Then go back
and do the same thing using a low-floating gray canvas dummy. You
should end up by having a dog who will keep in the channel until he runs
into a bird—a water-logged duck that he cannot see—or is stopped by the
whistle and cast to the shore. In training it is best to keep the dummies or
ducks out in the water, so that the dog will not tend to look for them on
the shore.

One thing to remember: if you can control your dog in a channel, you
will have him under control anyplace, so it is a worthwhile test to train on.
Its importance as a training test cannot be exaggerated.

Popping

Popping often comes from over-handling a sensitive dog. Any dog will
pop at times, but with an overly sensitive dog that is given too much
handling, it will become a bad fault. In this day of mechanical dogs, an
occasional pop is generally not dealt with too severely, except by the judge
looking for a way out. Some pops are legitimate, caused by a high wind
way out on a blind, or the rustle of brush or corn stalks. It is most natural
that a cooperative dog should have the tendency to pop or look for help,
to check himself occasionally; it is certainly an excusable fault under some
circumstances.

In training, one of the best ways to overcome it is to ignore it. When
the dog pops don't move, just out-wait him. Sometimes it takes a long
time. You wait, wait, wait, and then the dog gets tired of waiting. Maybe
he'll turn around and finally trot along. He is waiting for a cast, and if he
does not get it, he won't look for it as much. The next time, maybe you
won't have to wait so long. You can cure most dogs by just ignoring them
when they pop.

It sometimes helps if you call a dog back, punish him, and then send
him again. But this can become a definite pattern; it almost becomes a
game—go out 20 yards, pop, come back, get licked, and then go on. If you
see this pattern developing, try something different right away. Try

calling the dog back and just re-sending him without any punishment, or try re-sending him from the spot at which he popped.

But there is always the danger of getting the dog into the habit of a recast. I have had dogs who would go out and make one or two casts hunting for a bird, then quit and come back in. Some get in the habit of coming back for a recast on a blind. So perhaps it is better to settle for imperfection in the form of a poor line or an occasional pop than to strive for perfection, and call your dog back too often to re-send him.

If a dog is inclined to pop at the water's edge, I like to work him on a check cord so that I can pull him back to me if he pops. I punish him as his type requires and send him again. Maybe you'll have to give him a few licks on the rear, repeating the command "get back," before sending him again. If he is a very tough dog, the electric prod can be used instead of the whip. If the dog is inclined to run away from you, tie him on a 50- or 75-foot plastic rope and let him drag it.

With the more sensitive type of dog, just the threat of punishment and the fact that he is under control and can be pulled back if he stops is often enough to make him keep going.

I once had a dog who had the habit of looking back continually in the water, and I tried using the slingshot and a marble—but I never tried it again. A splash is the worst thing in the world; it defeats the purpose of the correction, and can make the popping worse. I don't think it is a good idea at all.

I used to have trouble with Firelei's Hornet—he would pop as he entered the water. Too many stones had been thrown, and after jumping into the water, he would wait in anticipation. Elmer LeGear loved to throw rocks for Hornet; it was a great game for them both. But later, in preparation for trials, it became a great problem.

There was a little round pond on Mr. Livingston's estate in Huntington, N.Y. I put dummies on one side, the first one about 10 feet back from the shore, and each succeeding one 10 feet farther back. Then I started Hornet 10 feet back from the opposite shore; and retired 10 feet farther back each time I sent him. The pond was about 60 feet across, so the first dummy meant an 80-foot retrieve, and the last one would be about 160 feet in all. It was a long, drawn-out battle.

At first I trained Hornet by this method early in the week, and on Wednesday I would have him doing it well, but a little down; so on Thursday and Friday, I would sweeten him up. That helped him to forget the unpleasantness of the lesson and, in the process, he also forgot the lesson.

By the trial he would be back in the same old rut, and after a great start, we had our humiliating failure: hop into the water, jump around, pop, pop, and finally out. Then I decided to reverse the process. I defied all the rules of good, sound training in my mind, and the boom was lowered just before the trial. I let him sleep on his lesson, and he worked perfectly the next day, won the trial, and finished his championship.

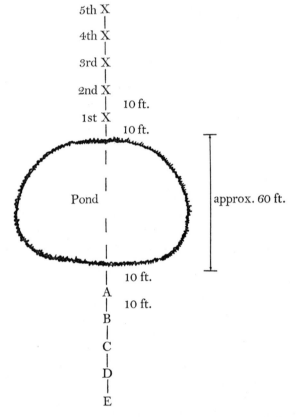

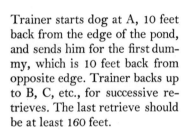

Trainer starts dog at A, 10 feet back from the edge of the pond, and sends him for the first dummy, which is 10 feet back from opposite edge. Trainer backs up to B, C, etc., for successive retrieves. The last retrieve should be at least 160 feet.

A great dog was Firelei's Hornet, with all the faults a dog could have and still be great. He had style and drive galore, along with a sticky delivery, and he was a breaker. But he was tough, and he never tired. He was a professional's dog. Discipline never slowed him up, and seldom even corrected him. I think he was the toughest Lab I ever had, with the most desire, whether for good or bad—and he always came back smiling.

On land, I think repetition, an awful lot of work—all-afternoon sessions, down the road, down the ditch, down the furrow, constant work—can do much to overcome popping.

And I have tried something that helped me on land blinds with Rosie (Cream City Co-ed). I have given her marked triples, a live bird and two dead birds, and then have sent her out on a blind first. She was so darned anxious to get back with the blind so that she could get the marks, that she just flew on the blind. Now if I'd done this early in her training, the results would have been just the contrary—she'd have been very confused. But now she understands, and that is the value of pattern training. She knew what was going to happen next, what the next chapter in the book was going to be, and she just flew out there. And then she righted herself, set herself up, and looked to go for the live bird.

Feel your way along carefully when trying to cure a dog of popping. If one method doesn't work try another, but be careful that in your search for perfection, you don't make the situation worse.

Placing Blind Retrieves

I have seen some very fine judges do some very queer things. One of the queerest is to have the bird on a blind covered up with dried leaves or grass. These judges are old hunters, and they want to be sure that the dog uses his nose. But under these conditions, how the hell can a dog use his nose to smell the bird? Scent from human hands and from the dogs who ran previously permeates the leaves and grass so much that, if the dog smells anything, you can rest assured that it is not a bird. If he has retrieved birds previously in that test, birds are what he is looking and smelling for. Human scent alone is much stronger than wild game scent; covering the bird only obliterates the bird scent. The test is to see how a dog will handle, but the dog proves his handling ability and then loses out because the bird has been obliterated. The bird should never be buried or concealed under human scent or the scent of other dogs.

Two other places not to put a blind: up a tree and down a hole.

Training Pete to Handle

Pete is two-and-a-half years old, just graduated from the Derby. He is fast and stylish, remembers and does doubles well, goes out fast and comes back fast, and is a marvelous moving dog. He is smart, friendly, affectionate, but soft; if you even act like you are going to get tough, he gets ready to bolt. I have been able to stop before this point is reached, and I must avoid this scene. He could be a great dog, but he will be hard to train to handle, it will be a slow job. I must give him the so-called "slow pitch," the "soft sell."

Pete always wants to be at heel; he was never taught to stay properly. Whenever he sits he wants to come to heel, so my first problem will be to get him to sit at the whistle right where he hears it. I say "stay" and move away from him, and he moves with me; I can hardly get behind him to give him a back cast. I give him "stay" drills with a long check cord around a post. Then I will get farther away from him, call him to me with the whistle and let him drag the cord, coming all the way to me. Then I'll slip the cord around a post, call him to me, and give him the whistle to stop as he hits the end of the cord, about halfway to me. When I can get him to stop promptly only a few feet from me, I will have made great progress.

Pete will be difficult to get to go out on a blind at all; he'll just refuse to go. So I'll put a dummy out in a road, walk away from it about 20 yards, then send him back, repeating this and increasing the distance. If he is still hesitant about going out on a blind, I'll have the bird boy throw a dummy just as he starts.

Soon I will start easing him into patterns. I'll put out blinds he can see, visible blinds, to the left. I'll give him a line to them. Then I'll give him a marked bird about 60 yards out in front, a line back to where the mark was (the bird boy put out a dummy when the dog wasn't looking), a line back to the blind on the left, and another line back to the mark. I'll give him a whistle half-way out on this one and, as he stops, a cast to the blind on the left. It's a guess system, but it works well on sensitive, eager dogs like Pete, who want to please.

When he has learned his left cast, I'll work on the right. Perhaps I'll put blinds out to the right and sit Pete about 20 yards away to the left of the blind, back away from him, and give him the right over. The next time I'll put him 40 yards away, retire farther back, and cast him. I'll do this until I am 60 yards from him. Then I'll put the bird boy out about 70 yards, bring Pete to heel, give him a mark straight ahead, and repeat this line as a semi-blind to a dummy that the bird boy drops while Pete is on his way in with the mark. The next time, I'll send him straight ahead with no dummy out there, give him the stop whistle and a back cast, and have the dummy thrown by the bird boy as Pete looks back. Then I'll send him out again, stop him, and give a right cast to the pile of blinds, walking in that direction to help him. I'll end up each time with complete lines to the right or left and straight out. On a long blind, a semi-blind that he knows is there, sometimes I'll send him, stop him, call him part way in with the whistle, stop him again, and give him a back cast.

I have had some wonderful handling dogs who were trained this way and who never were whipped, shot, or prodded. It is recommended for particularly shy or soft dogs who won't take any form of punishment. Sometimes you can start a dog this way and gradually work into the more orthodox systems that demand a little more pressure.

Today I worked Pete three times. The sessions must be short and frequent. He wants to run to his pen, but I am patient and don't chase him or don't punish him; I bring him back to the spot he bolted from, and give him the whistle there again.

He will come along, but very slowly. It will be four or five months of patient drill with no rough stuff before appreciable gains are made. After he does learn to stop with some consistency, maybe a slingshot or bird shot can be used carefully and cautiously when he ignores the whistle. If the results are good, maybe even a shotgun can be tried, at a proper distance. But I must start on the rough stuff carefully, with judgement; and if his reaction is bad, I stop it. I must feel my way very gradually, give him lots of praise when he does well and not let him get down too much.

If you have a dog like Pete, I warn you—it will be slow. I worry more about you than the dog. If you take things in your stride, keep working and don't blow your top, he will come. There will be discouraging moments and setbacks, but don't let it bother you; tomorrow might not be as good as today, but measure his progress in weeks or months.

Editors' note: This is Sage's Saskeram Pete, owned by Dr. Richard Keskey, who ran in the '66 National. When this chapter was written Pete was still a youngster and in this stage of training. Charley's approach to this dog's problems paid off.

The Dogs

Does a Dog Think?

I don't give dogs much credit for thinking, that is, for being able to reason out a problem. I believe they are more creatures of habit, with some highly developed senses and instincts. These senses often make us think that a dog can think or reason. If we could exchange a portion of our thinking powers for the dog's senses, we would probably be credited with being smarter than we are—and the senses would probably be more valuable to us than the small power of thinking we gave up.

Mr. Pomeroy used to come out to see Sweepy Boy (Bracken Sweep), and old Sweepy Boy could recognize the sound of his motor; he sensed his approach. And I know that he always knew which pocket Mr. Pomeroy's crunchons were in. An old man in my cabin in Missouri used to say that his dog, Smokey, not only knew what he was thinking, but what he was going to think. If we watch two coyotes stalking a rabbit in South Dakota, we'll see that one goes back to the rabbit hole and waits while the other one chases the rabbit in the opposite direction. The rabbit circles to its hole, and is caught by the waiting coyote.

Dogs have tremendous homing instincts. When lost, they are able to find their way back amazingly well. Never leave the place where you have lost a dog. If you cannot stay there yourself, leave someone else there, or an open car; unless something happens to him, he will find his way back.

A dog's instincts are so great that they are hard for us to understand or define. Dogs have been known to meet buses at a certain time every day, except on the one day a week that the bus does not run.

But in training I think we must assume that a dog's behavior is based on association rather than thought, and I work on the theory that repetition builds up that association. I don't want to close all doors to the idea that a dog can think, but I certainly don't want to depend on his ability to reason to get results.

Dogs do have a certain amount of intelligence, but I don't believe that they can use it to make comparisons or deductions. Some dogs are able to grasp things and catch on more quickly than others, but whether they are smart or the others are just sluggish, I don't know. Some dogs seem to try to figure you out; they are curious and inquisitive, and it certainly makes them more biddable and tractable. Some dogs seem to want to please, and this has a lot to do with it. This quality is developed to a great extent in early training. You get over to them the idea that you are pleased, that they have done something you like, and you repay them for it, give them a crunchon. You are happy, you register being happy, and I think that a dog senses this.

A dog certainly senses it when you are not happy. I used to have a bitch who would almost stop when she got about 10 feet from me, and I would have to put a silly grin on my face. That was Sodak Gypsy Queen, a little Chesapeake. I would just grin, and then she would come on in. If I did not put on a pleased look, why she would stop completely.

Some dogs move faster when they know they have pleased you. Of course, different trainers have different degrees of ability to put this over to their dogs.

Maybe it's all in the nervous system. We've seen dumb dogs and smart dogs, aggressive dogs and spooky dogs. Maybe the spooky dog's ancestors were outcasts who were beaten by the pack, and maybe the aggressive, mean dog had forebears who learned early to depend on their brawn, and thus became tougher and more muscular. Perhaps another type had to depend on cunning and became quicker and sharper, with a keener intellect and keener senses.

In training, the ones with the right balance of brawn and the keener senses—a balance of aggressiveness and sensitivity—just fall in line quicker. The brawny type will not run away and can take punishment. The shrewder type, with his sensitivity and alertness—the little pup who cocks his head—will by nature respond to training faster; he just seems to learn faster.

These seemingly bright dogs catch on to lots of things faster. While judging the first trial in Omaha, I asked Gene Whelan what he had put in his book when a certain dog ran down the shore of the Missouri River and then jumped in and swam out to the duck rather than angling directly into the river from his handler, as we train them to do now, or try to. "Oh boy," replied Gene, "I gave that dog extra credit; he is river-wise." The dogs who are not river-wise, the ones who jump right in and swim directly out to the spot where a duck hits the water, will never get the duck. Yes sir, on the Platte and Missouri Rivers, where they do lots of hunting, if you don't have a river-wise dog, you lose lots of ducks. The old hunting dogs tear down the river bank with one eye on the river until the fast floating duck is spotted, and then the old-timers, the real river-wise dogs, go beyond it before plunging in, so that they will be out there to meet the duck.

A man once brought me a dog to cure of the habit of getting into his car and becoming very possessive, very mean. The dog wouldn't let anyone even start to enter the car; he'd tear him to pieces. I asked the owner, "Why do you want him cured of that? He seems like a wonderful watch dog. You should want him to do that; what a fine thing for a dog to do." But it turned out that sometimes the dog would get into the wrong car. Recently he had left his owner's car and gotten into a car across the street, and by the time his owner returned, an immense crowd had gathered. There were policemen and firemen, all coaxing and threatening, while the crowd was yelling, jeering and ridiculing. It was the policemen's car that the dog was in, and the police told the owner that if he didn't turn the dog over to a professional trainer at once and break him of the habit, that they would shoot the dog. It was only on the promise that the dog would be brought to me that the owner was allowed to keep him.

Well, I trained him not to get into cars, to go by cars without any attempt to get in. The cure probably worked like a charm for about two weeks. If the dog could have been sent back to someone else, the problem would probably have been solved permanently; but when a dog is sent back to his original owner, the problem usually starts up again quickly. The old cues start it, the old associations that started it in the first place; the old habits return.

Many remarkable things have been credited to dogs. Sometimes, no doubt, they are true, but many are the figment of someone's imagination.

Do Dogs Work in Cycles?

I do think that dogs tend to work in cycles. They have their ups and downs just like baseball players. We probably go along with them, maybe even help them into their slumps—or maybe we can bring them out. I notice that when you win a trial, it is generally followed by another good trial. It sometimes looks as if it is a reflection on us. When the dogs get to doing poor work, and we get on them a little too much, they get down; when we have a good trial and are pretty happy, we let up on the dogs and let them coast a bit.

Dogs sometimes go into slumps through overwork or through a lack of variation in their work, the monotony of it all. At times it looks like we may work them too hard. Maybe we are a little too tense ourselves, and if we get to losing we just get more tense; maybe we just need to loosen ourselves up a bit.

A fighter would never train for a fight by doing nothing but fighting. He sharpens his punching with the light bag, and his hard punching with the heavy bag; if he is going to fight a defensive fight, he shadow boxes a lot; and he does lots of road work for stamina. He isn't trained to be able to take a beating by getting lots of beatings. Instead of toughening him up, after a certain point that would soften him up.

To get a dog ready for a trial, it is not so much what you do as what you don't do that counts. Don't train too much on tests that you are apt to get at a trial—that would be like a fighter training for a fight by fighting. Don't ignore them entirely, but use them in moderation and at the proper time, with full consideration of each dog's strengths and weaknesses. I have found that one day a week is sufficient for the crazy or unorthodox tests that you think you may get at the trials. Most dogs have a way of grasping the wrong ideas quickly from tests like these. Also, it is not a good idea to keep your dogs continually confused. Try to have your dogs creatures of habit—good habits—rather than creatures of fear.

Don't lay out the same test for all your dogs if you have a group. For some dogs, certain tests are suicide. Every test should be changed slightly to suit the individual dog's needs, weaknesses and strengths. Sometimes the entire test can be changed just by the trainer changing his location. You would be surprised how much shifting a few feet can change the picture. When you have a lot of dogs to work, it is difficult to change the set-up by moving the bird boys for each dog, so just move yourself.

Too many short distraction birds thrown at a dog just add to his confusion. That is what they are for in a trial, to confuse a dog, so beware of too many short diversion birds in training.

You can't make your dog strong on everything, so try to make him strong on the things that are apt to pay off; play the percentages. Avoid certain tests that might win you one particular trial. Remember, unless it is the National, you are training for the whole season. A tendency to run the shore line might win you one trial, but it will lose you more in the long run. You have to take a chance on some tests. Generally it is better for your dog to have a tendency to overrun a short mark than to hunt short on a long mark.

As a rule, good training boils down to balance, correct proportion, in all its aspects—balance betweeen discipline and relaxation, between demanding tests and pattern running, short marks and long marks. Try to think what kind of habits your dog is getting into.

Don't demand perfection; in an intense effort to get perfection, you could end up with very little. It is mighty good training, usually, to settle for work that is a little short of perfection. The height of folly is to strive for perfection by returning a dog continually to the same mark or the same blind, until he pin-points it. He gets a mania to return to the spot where he has been, and you can't line him up for a line that is even close to his last retrieve. He always figures that you are returning him to the last fall. He has been made to do it a million times, so why shouldn't he? If you are going to repeat a test, always try and do something else in between so that the dog isn't returning continually to the same fall. A constant demand for perfection can really discourage a dog, and he may never be able to loosen up enough to get into a good cycle. Don't expect to be able to keep a dog in top form all the time—it can't be done.

If a dog has a chronic fault, the usual procedure is to get in a good correction, knock the dog down early in the week before a trial, and then spend the rest of the week sweetening him up. Is this wise? Sometimes it is, but at other times the sweetening-up becomes a form of apology. By the time the dog is sweetened up, he has forgotten the lesson and is right back in his old groove. Certainly, for some types of dogs, the later the correction is made the better, and you take a chance that the field trial atmosphere in the first series will be sufficient to make him forget his dejected mood without forgetting the lesson as well.

In the old days, I used to see a certain trainer watch the first series and then rush away in his car. Then you'd hear a distant shot—but he had the knack of getting back just before he was called to the line. His dogs were hard to beat. If it was a handling test, they were especially sharp, and if it was a rugged staunching test, they were especially staunch. No doubt, he felt that the closer the correction could be to the series, the more effective it was. He was hard to beat. In the big last series, he was usually very impressive.

Firelei's Hornet had the bad habit of refusing to continue on his line into the water. He would go in just so far and pop, and a second command was always necessary. My policy had been to give him the works on Monday, not pull any punches, and then spend the rest of the week sweetening him up. By trial time Saturday I would have him sweet all right, but he was right back where he had been before Monday's lesson. After several unsuccessful weeks of this procedure, I decided to reverse the process. I put the pressure on him at the last moment, on Friday afternoon. There was no sweetening-up process. What were the results? He won the trial. I have decided that for this particular type of tough and eager dog, it was the right process; for another type, it might not be. Every dog must be dealt with differently, so you must know your dog.

A dog, when punished, should be punished effectively, even severely, but not often. Don't punish a dog mildly and frequently—this becomes nagging. And don't pet a dog immediately after punishing him—this is construed as an apology. Wouldn't it be better to let him sleep on it for awhile before the sweetening-up process begins?

Dogs must have some fun periods when they can romp and play with their trainer, when every movement of his hand or arm is not interpreted as a threatening gesture. A dog must know and be told the time for his relaxation periods and the time for serious training, his study periods. It's important that a trainer have the ability to say and get over to the dog, "Now we're getting down to serious business. It's the work hour; all smelling and puttering around is off; pay attention." It is not a "please," but a *must*. How do you get a dog on the beam? If he is indifferent, grab him and shake him up like you would a son, whose love and respect were not gained by letting him have his way too much—or by too many rough sessions, either. There is a definite time for each kind of period, and a definite signal and approach. The right balance between play time and work time is a key to keeping your dog working sharply, well controlled, yet still relaxed and happy.

Normally, the ideal schedule for training the older trial dogs is to do the tough stuff and the unorthodox tests early in the week, and then drop off to singles, relax the pressure, and sweeten them up if necessary before the trial. If you can learn how to get a dog down at the right time so that he will be up at the right time, then you have solved one of the mysteries of canine life. The perfect dog is the one who wants to do one thing, but can be made to do another, who wants to go his way, but knows he must go your way.

It takes a well-planned training schedule to keep this balance in a dog. Don't decide what you will do at the last moment as you go out for a training session. Plan it days in advance, weeks in advance—yes, months and even years in advance—until you reach the dog's maturity. Your plans and schedules will often be upset and have to be revised, but keep on planning anyway. The trainer who comes closest to planning an orderly life in the training of his dogs is the one who will win the most trials.

One of the secrets of training is not trying for perfection; a certain amount of tolerance is necessary. Recognize the strengths and weaknesses of your dog, and don't try too hard to overcome the weaknesses or you may lose the strengths. When a dog is really running well don't try too hard to improve his weak points, or you may upset the whole balance.

Getting Ready for the National

To get a dog ready for the National, I like to start several weeks before the trial, at least two weeks ahead, and give corrective work-outs. I plan the tests and the length of time I'll work according to the dog's particular problems, weaknesses, and temperament. The tests are open invitations for him to make mistakes, because I want to correct him severely enough to last until the big trial is over. As different dogs reach their peaks at different times, only the trainer can figure just when a dog will be at the right point to start these corrective tests.

During this period, besides putting all the pressure on the dog that I think he needs, I like to work him on unorthodox tests, the kind you don't ordinarily get—maybe four or five marks at a time, or picking up a blind before the marks, tests like that.

But I try to avoid any trouble within a week of the trial. I don't think you should carry severe training right up to the last minute. You want the dog to be in top shape physically, but also loose and relaxed, so that he can mark well. One of the greatest attributes a competitor can have is the ability to relax. Joe Louis, I'm told, would almost fall asleep in the dressing room before a fight. Sheltercove Beauty ran a wonderful National in 1944, and she would almost go to sleep on line while honoring. That used to aggravate me a bit, but Dr. Evans, her owner, said it was a wonderful attribute.

So, I'll stick to the orthodox tests—triples and doubles, maybe an occasional blind—but nothing that might get the dog into serious trouble. Exaggerate these tests a little to keep the dog in good habits. For example, keep the water blinds well out in the water, all floating, off points, away from the rushes, across the islands, always over, through, or beyond. Give a minimum number of birds in the rushes or on points. Exaggerate the lines so that the dog has to keep going long distance, over dikes, across roads, over ridges and ditches, even through fences; keep him going, never letting him stop until he finds a bird.

Then, during the last three or four days before the big trial, I like to give nothing but singles on dummies. I think it is the greatest training for marking in the world to keep a dog's head from swinging. The dog is singled to the point that his head, eyes, and thoughts never switch until another shot is fired: his concentration is 100 percent on that dummy. Sometimes I put three sets of guns out, but I always give singles, using the guns one at a time and varying the sequence. The dog may start looking poorly, he may get down, and it may be hard for you to keep from getting discouraged with him; but remember, the trial atmosphere will bring him up again in a hurry. If he is an outlaw, I would vary this program, and try to lay out a test that will promote a brawl on the morning before the trial.

The day before the trial, or the morning of the trial, if you have a potential breaker or a bad creeper, if you have dog who gets terribly high and needs settling, you may want to use birds. If you have a dog who needs building up or mellowing down, long shot birds may help. You must know your dog and his needs, but don't be too discouraged if he loses interest and slows up after a spell of singles on dummies. He will come to life on birds at the trial.

Some dogs do better with a little work early in the morning before a trial. When I won the National with Tamarack, I gave him two or three singles every morning before I went over to the trial grounds, and he never did pin-point one of them. An hour later, at the trial, he marked perfectly. Well, he'd already had three lousy marks under his belt, so maybe that helped to settle him, maybe it took just the right amount of edge off him.

Some of the tremendously high dogs always need a series or two before the trial. I think Tony Berger used to run Cork ('55 Nat. Ch. Cork of Oakwood Lane) hard before he ran him in the National.

What is the stupidest thing you can do in preparation for the big one? Training on actual trial tests; trying to think what those particular judges might give, and pouring those tests down the dog's throat with plenty of birds. It's been my experience that the dog so prepared won't have a chance—he is out before you start.

For example, if you knew that you were going to get a blind in which
the dog had to swim parallel to a shoreline for 100 yards and the duck
would be on the land, what would happen if you trained on this? The next
time you sent your dog on this blind, he would want to land 75 yards down,
and you might have a hard time keeping him from landing 50 or even 25
yards down the shore. He just wouldn't want to go all the way by water,
and it would be a continuous fight. So keep your blinds well out in the
water, never in the rushes or on points or islands; do these things in
exaggerated form.

When I train with a group, and just before the trial someone says "do
this," "do that," "this trainer always gives this kind of test," or "that
judge will always call for such-and-such a test," I always want to go somewhere else to train. As Cotton Pershall says, if your dog can mark and will
do what you tell him, you need not worry about the tests.

Most important of all, of course, is knowing your individual dog;
knowing when you should train him and when you shouldn't; how much
you should train him, and on what kind of tests; when you should get on
him and when you shouldn't; when he should be exercised and when he
should be played with; and even when he should be fed and watered.

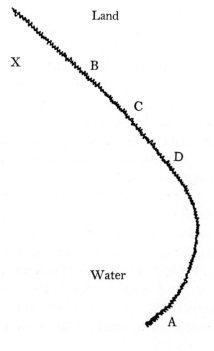

The trainer starts the dog on the water blind
from A. If the bird is on land at B, the dog
will tend to land at C, or even at D, if this
blind is repeated, or on a similar water blind.
In training, put the bird out in the water at
X, so that dog will not tend to go ashore.

I remember Black Boy (Black Boy XI) when Ray Staudinger had him. He was a pretty temperamental dog, and I wondered how well Ray would get on with him. Well, when I was East training with Ray, he would get the dog out of the car and then put him back without training him, saying, "It won't do any good; it will do him more harm than good; he isn't right to train now." Sometimes some of the boys might have thought Ray was putting on a little act. But Ray had wonderful success with that dog, and he certainly knew him well, knew how to get the best out of him. I think it was one of the best jobs of training and handling of all time.

Conditioning for a trial is very important. A dog must be in top physical shape—wind, muscle and spirit—without being stale. Hardening up a dog by retrieves will not do; by the time you have the dog in physical shape, he is stale, sour, overworked. Some trainers like to run their dogs behind a car a lot when they can get a dirt road or a prairie to run on. Swimming behind a boat in packs, as well as running in packs, is good, too. They harden up and sharpen up at the same time when they run together.

There is no question that the dog who is really ready for a big trial is on the threshold of committing grave mistakes. His eagerness may put him on the border line of serious faults—bad line manners, creeping, maybe even breaking—but he can do great dog work. Eagerness makes the marking. A dog who is high, almost too eager, may mark very well.

On the other hand, a dog who is almost too down in training, on the verge of doing everything wrong, may be just right for the trial. He has not lost the meaning of the whistle, and it is in his mind almost to the point where he pops, but he does not pop. He'll take your line, maybe with his spirits down a little at the start, but he'll keep going and gather speed. "Up enough not to pop, down enough not to break"—that is the way you want him. When you can get him that way, you are hard to beat, but when you go too far one way or the other, all hell will fall in on you.

A good handler knows when he has got a dog to this point in training, but there is an element of guesswork, and they don't always guess right.

I have seen dogs with fine handlers look terrible in training, and the handler said, "Now I have got him; that's just the way I want him." And he was right—the dog made a complete change of form in the trial and was hard to beat. An inexperienced trainer after a miserable training session like that would have gone home and beaten his wife.

Tony Berger, with whom I trained for the '63 National which he won with Coly ('61 & '63 Nat. Ch. Del-Tone Colvin), knew just how much hard training and how much sweetening-up his dogs needed. Tony would say, "Coly is mad," or "Trouble (Beautywood's Rare Trouble) is mad," or "Mike (Raven Mike of Stonegate) is sulking," and he'd give them the old fun period, letting them break, not holding them. The subdued dogs entered right into the spirit of it, and they jumped around like pups. They forgot they were mad, and a dismal training session ended in fun and relaxation. Now, Tony guessed right this time with Coly, who won, and he was great with Trouble, who completed even though he had looked poorly in training.

If I have gathered any good ideas about training in 30 years experience, it's this preparation for the big one. With one dog, I might go out in the first series, or in the third. But give me a group of four or five, and you can safely bet that one of them will be knocking on the door and that the others could have come close. I can't beat Lady Luck by this method, but if Lady Luck does not turn her back on me, I'll wager that one of my group will be in there fighting at the end.

The Three Breeds

I have heard trainers say that to train a Chesapeake you should use an elm club instead of a whip, to train a Lab use a whip, and to train a Golden use a wet kleenex. This is meant to represent the different degrees of toughness of the three breeds. I have not found this to be so. I have often found that the Chesapeake can be very soft, the Golden can sometimes be very tough, and the Lab can be either. It's all up to the individual dog.

But as a rule, I think the generally accepted opinion that the average Golden is a little more sensitive, and that you can't be and don't need to be as tough with him in training, is correct. As far as a Golden being a sissy is concerned—that is wrong. They are certainly able to defend themselves in a dog fight. Ben Boalt's Stilrovin Nitro Express, and The Golden Kidd, one of Mariel King's outstanding Goldens, were two of the worst fighters I ever had—or could be if they got started—but they were not troublemakers. The Golden is probably a little quicker to learn, a little quicker to catch on, and I don't think they need as much pressure. I do think the picture should be kept a little rosier for them because they need a little more encouragement. Generally, you can't be as severe with them as you can be with a Lab. There are exceptions, of course, but it is the rule and not the exception that I am talking about.

The Labs are classy dogs, biddable, tractable dogs, and a little tougher

than the average Golden. You can get on them a little more, and they are
nice dogs to train. I don't think you are as likely to have as many temperamental or other problems with a Lab as you might with a Golden or a
Chesapeake.

The Chesapeake is considered to be the toughest of all the retriever
breeds. They are thought to be fighters—mean, vicious and all that. But
in my experience, that is absolutely not so. They are very sensitive and
affectionate dogs. I think they are often one-man dogs because they have
been used more for meat hunting and as companions. They have been
raised and used as meat-getters by the single hunter who wants a dog.
The boy out in the Dakotas or down on the Eastern Shore is going to get
a Chesapeake, as a rule, and he's going to hunt with the dog himself, and
give it whatever training is necessary himself. They don't go to trials, but
this is his dog, isn't it? They are hunting buddies, and the dog becomes
possessive. He resents any outsider, dog or human, coming between him
and his buddy. They say the Chesapeake has a hard mouth. I don't know
that this is so, but they are probably a little more rugged, and their biting
power is probably a little greater. The Chesapeake is a very affectionate
dog, and I don't think that they are necessarily mean or looking for trouble
at all. I have had more timid, soft Chesapeakes, I believe, than I have had
timid Labs or Goldens.

I have never had any of the dogs of the retriever breeds bite me
viciously. I have been bitten by dogs I was trying to separate in a fight,
and by dogs caught in fences, and by injured dogs, but I have never been
bitten viciously.

Of course, the Labs were imported into this country by people with
money. Mr. Carlisle, Mr. Marshall Field, and Mr. Harriman brought
them over. The early importers and breeders of Labs in the East were
people who could afford to give a lot of study to the selection, breeding,
and care of their dogs. They had experts handling their dogs, raising them
and training them. I think the Labs had a little better start. I think they
got into the hands of people who would exploit them more and see to it
that they had the proper care and training.

The Chesapeake went to the little fellow in Dakota; that is where I got
acquainted with them. We hunted a lot with them. We didn't know much
about them. They slept in the barn and were fed table scraps, and some of
them weren't fed at all. They didn't have the proper bringing-up or training, and they didn't have the opportunities that the Labs, or even the
Goldens, have had.

Tony Bliss, in the East, had money, and he gave his Chesapeakes the proper care, the proper opportunities. I think he was getting someplace with them, developing a fine strain of the breed, when he more or less got away from it. It was a long, drawn-out process, and I think he was beginning to get results about the time that he gave up on it.

The Chesapeake and the Golden probably make a fine dog for the amateur, who can give more individual time, attention, and loving care to his dog. The Lab fits into a pro's type of training better; he is a more satisfactory dog for a pro to train.

Maybe the Lab has developed his hearty, hale-fellow-well-met attitude from working in the social groups at the exclusive clubs. Maybe the Golden has been used so much as a house dog, with women training and handling him, that he has become more sensitive and susceptible to feminine charm. He's used to being treated with loving affection, and at least gives the outward appearance of softness. And the Chesapeake has been used so much by the individual hunter as a constant companion and meat-getter, that he has developed a lone-wolf attitude.

The Chesapeake is a rugged hunter with a patch in his pants; the Lab a sporty hunter with feathers in his hat; and the Golden, with a woman's care, expects love, kindness, and applied psychology—methods above the ordinary man's ability to understand and use.

I try to train them all as the particular dog warrants, and not as the breed—or somebody's idea of the breed—might suggest. It is all up to the individual dog; each one needs a different approach. And you can't always tell the first day out, for dogs sometimes have fronts like humans, concealing a very different interior.

Should You Train Dogs and Bitches Differently?

On the whole, I train the females and the males in about the same way, but I do find that there are some general differences.

I think that females come along a little faster and learn a little faster, but reach their saturation point faster, too. The male will come along more slowly, but may finally catch up and possibly surpass the female. Eventually, the male is likely to progress a little farther.

The female requires a little less harsh treatment; she fits into my type of training better than the male. The average female is a little softer, maybe, and a little more responsive to rewards, pats, crunchons, etc. She is

given to moods, is a little more temperamental than the male. Females
have their times when they are coming in season, they have their cycles to
go through, physical changes and temperamental changes. With some
females, you just don't know whether they are going to be off or on.

Mag ('45 Nat. Ch. Black Magic of Audlon) was crazy about retrieving; it was a mania with her, and I never saw her any different, never saw
any changes in her. But Sheltercove Beauty ('44 Nat. Ch.) was a little
temperamental; there were times when she just seemed very uninterested.
I would have to get out and shake her up a little, and then she'd be all right.
She was almost like a small boy; she had to be scolded, chucked under the
chin, and told, "Don't forget to do this; now get on the beam." I'd grab her
and just give her a little shaking, set her down, and she'd be an entirely
different dog. All trainers have had dogs of that type, dogs you have to
get on a little before they will work—but I think that it's a matter of the
individual dog and not the sex.

On the whole, a female is more inclined to be upset by a licking than a
male, and will probably remain upset a little longer. But there are also very
masculine females who are tougher than males, and need more of a pounding. And of course there are soft males, too.

Males are more inclined to trail and smell, and their minds are more
easily diverted than those of females. They are slower to progress in their
training at first, but don't give up too soon on the slower-developing male.

The females, who progress more rapidly, reach their peak sooner and
may fade out at an earlier age. They are inclined to slow up a little sooner
and to lose some interest as they get older. There seem to be more sluggish
old females than sluggish old males; it is probably a physical condition.

While females are not the fighters that males are, or as easily diverted
by smells, I think on the whole that they give you more problems to
contend with than males do. So don't carry a female too long; expect her
to progress faster and show signs of brilliance sooner.

Breeding a Young Dog

When it comes to deciding the time to breed a bitch, I think only the
owner can decide whether to breed her young or wait until she is older. If
she is a good working bitch, one who shows real promise, you will have
to face the fact that it may take three months or so out of her training and
trial career. She can probably run for a month after she is bred, but that

leaves another month in whelp, and it will be about two months before the pups are weaned and the bitch is dried up enough to run again.

On the other hand, I don't think you should wait too long, because an old bitch is more likely to have trouble than a young one. Some people say you shouldn't breed a good working bitch, that you don't get really good bitches too often, and that having a litter of pups will ruin a bitch, slow her up and make her lazy. Well, I don't think it's necessarily so that breeding must slow up a bitch. You have to watch her diet carefully and keep up the exercise. If you just let her lie around and get sloppy, then she probably will slow up, but this doesn't have to happen.

The same thing is true of a spayed bitch. In the Army, the only bitches they used were spayed, and they stayed in good condition. Their diets were watched carefully and they got plenty of exercise. So there is no reason to let a bitch get fat and lazy just because she has been spayed or has had a litter. Firelei of Deer Creek had a big litter, and several weeks later she did well in the trials.

I have not noticed that the good bitches fade out any faster after having a litter. In some cases, I think it has actually improved the bitch. She gets a little more possessive, a little more bold, and is not as soft or as timid as she might have been before. I suppose a protective instinct is developed while she is with her young, and it helps to give her a new toughness.

Just be sure to watch a bitch's diet carefully, especially when you are drying her up after weaning. Don't let her go on feeding her pups too long, and cut down on her feed as soon as you safely can.

As to a young male, there are several factors to keep in mind when deciding the proper time to start using him at stud. If the dog's interest in birds and retrieving is a little less than you'd like, if he doesn't really have an excess of desire, I think I'd be a little hesitant to breed him young. You might be taking a chance on his getting over-sexed. He may end up more interested in smelling after the bitches than in birds. Of course, this type of dog isn't generally going to make a great trial dog, anyway.

Yet, I have noticed very young dogs who were not affected in the least by being bred. And I have had dogs who were used extensively at stud without it hurting them at all. Sodak Rip, who wasn't easy to breed, Nelgard's King Tut, and The Spider of Kingswere, all were pretty much the same—it didn't seem to affect them one way or another.

An older male dog who hasn't been bred before sometimes has difficulty breeding. It's hard to tell whether they lack the desire to breed or the know-how, but it is a good thing to keep in mind. Also, if you wait until a dog is four years old to breed him, it will be another two years before the pups are proven, and you do not have much chance to profit from this mating if it should prove to be a great one. If your dog should turn out to be a fine stud dog, you want as many years as possible to use him. If a particular breeding turns out to be exceptionally good, you would like a chance to repeat it, both for the sake of the breed and your pocketbook. This is also something to keep in mind when deciding the time to breed a bitch. If she should turn out to be a great producer, you would like to be able to get more litters from her.

Selecting a Sire

If I am going to pick a sire for a particular bitch, I first go over her strong points and her weak points. I look for a sire who can produce the qualities that I think my bitch needs. I want to see what the sire can produce; that is more important than what he is like himself. If my bitch is too small or too soft, she needs to be bred to a sire who can produce size and toughness.

If it is size I am interested in, and I want pups bigger than my bitch, I want to see the size of the pups this particular sire produces. I have known big sires to produce little pups, and little sires who produced big pups. So it is his potential as a producer, rather than the dog himself, that I am interested in.

I might look around to find a dog I really liked, a dog who has all the qualities I think my bitch needs, and then go to his sire. If the sire turns out to be a poor type of dog, undersized or unsound, I will be hesitant to breed to him. I want him to be of good type and, most important of all, to be a proven producer of good types. I'd check to see that he wasn't the only one of his line who has the good qualities I am looking for, and I'd check as many of his progeny as I can to be sure that the pup I like isn't an exception, a fluke. I'd also like to check the different bitches he has bred, to be sure that two or three good specimens have come out of all of the litters. To get two or three good ones out of a litter is a good percentage, I think. If he has been able to produce two or three good specimens in each of several litters, if most of his pups are good and only a few are poor, I would say he is a well-proven sire.

Also, I would like to have a dog with a good name and record, one who comes from good, proven blood lines, because this helps in selling the pups—after all, I eat. If you plan to go on with the breeding, it is usually easier to perpetuate a good line of dogs.

I like to go back three generations in the pedigree, look at the grandsire and granddam, and be sure they too have the qualities I want.

These are the qualities I am looking for: 1) type, including size, which I think is very important—too small a dog has a handicap; 2) style, including speed, hunting ability, nose, birdiness, pick-up, and style in the water; and 3) intelligence and temperament, including good disposition, boldness, alertness, will to please, lack of spookiness or belligerence—all the things that suggest brains and tractability. I want a preponderance of one good trait to overcome a shortcoming in another; I would permit a weakness in one, if there was great strength in another. If a dog is short of one virtue, but is so terrific in his other qualities as to make him an outstanding dog, I might still be interested. But my bitch's shortcomings must not be along the same lines; she must be strong in the areas where he is weak. A dog who had a pronounced weakness would have to have terrific qualities in other ways before I would want to breed to him.

Good type may not be absolutely necessary, but it is highly desirable. To have a winner who is a poor specimen of the breed, and have everyone want to breed to him, is tragic. I remember old Hi-Tail (Hi-Tail of Wyandotte)—a brilliant dog. He had everything, including a tail that curled over his back, which was the subject of joking and ridicule. "Well," Dave Elliot, his handler, would say, "I don't care about his tail; he doesn't retrieve with his tail." It is true that he had great qualities we want to carry on, but type just can't be ignored for future breeding.

CHAPTER 7

Trials, Trainers, Handlers and Judges

How Trials Have Changed

Trials have changed tremendously since 1936, when the first trial was held in the Midwest. We have gone through various cycles—fads possibly—when different phases of dog work were emphasized. And competition has become much tougher. We have more good dogs, better training, and more fine handlers.

In the old days, your dog had to be a good marker without question, and a good hunting dog. Then the judge would say, "Now that we've found your dog can mark and hunt, let's see if he will handle with the whistle." So you would work him on a blind down a road or a cowpath, maybe fifty or sixty yards. You would blow your whistle a couple of times, stop him a couple of times, and if he'd stop and take directions at all, well, he'd handle. And the trial was over—that was all. It was just a test to see if he would handle after a fashion, and it was unheard of to count the number of whistles or take note of the directions of the casts. The gallery and handlers, meanwhile, were complaining about the mechanical test.

The water tests were usually short, through decoys into open water. In '34, the tests were through live decoys. In Derbies, especially, water was not emphasized much. Derby dogs might be given just one duck in the decoys, but on land they would have more difficult doubles and singles. The early Chesapeake trials, however, liked to emphasize the water work. Now, the balance between land and water is usually fairly good. But, of course, time can be a factor, for water tests take longer.

It was very important that your dog be absolutely staunch. The judges threw staunching tests at you right up to the very end; in fact, I think the staunching tests got worse as the trial went on. These days, it looks as if most judges are trying to avoid a break in the last two or three series. They

Ernest Burton, Bernard Genty, Charley Morgan and J. Gould Remick at the National Retriever Trial, Herrin, Illinois, December 5–7, 1947. *Photograph: Evelyn M. Shafer.*

Howes Burton, Charley Morgan and James Lamb Free discuss a test, while His Majesty The Buck, owned by Mr. J. Hubert, peeks at the photographer. Women's Field Trial Club, Westhampton Beach, L.I., New York, November 12–14, 1948. *Photograph: Evelyn M. Shafer.*

don't like to see a dog break who is leading in the trial, and I agree with that.

Back in the late '30s and early '40s, if your dog just stood up fast, it was considered a break. I had a dog thrown out of a trial in the East for standing up on line. And as for creeping, that was completely out, that's all—it was a break. Now we've gotten so that a dog can stand up and creep ahead. There are very few real staunching tests thrown anymore.

Today, dogs usually run and then honor, and that takes a little of the edge off a dog. He goes up on line and he runs, and then he'll relax, won't he, while he honors the other dog running. Back in those days, you came up on line in braces, and you might run first or second. Sometimes there were more than two on line, maybe as many as six, and you might run sixth.

I was running Bob Sawbridge's dog, Boar Ranch Nip, at Eagle with Ned Dodge judging, and my dog broke. I said, "My lands, Ned, I didn't think you would ever call my number." Ned said, "I could see he was going to break, so I held him." They thought that was permissible in those days, for a judge to hold a dog if it looked like he was going to break. They would almost wait until he did break.

The marking was much more difficult then. As a rule, they didn't avoid heavy cover. They purposely went to heavy cover, where you couldn't see your dog, not even get a glimpse of him. There wasn't any question of handling him—you couldn't possibly.

Of course, they keep talking about that today, talking about making the marking tests tougher. But the more they talk about it, the less they get away from the handling, the mechanical end of it, and back to the real marking, the real hunting tests.

Then, along in the early '40s, we began to have a few really fine handling dogs—Mr. Bakewell's Golden, Rip, for example. It almost seemed as if Mr. Bakewell would intentionally handle him on a mark to prove that the dog could do it. The mere fact that he would handle, and handle so beautifully, did impress the judges in those days.

Later on, when I got Mr. Pomeroy's dogs from Cotton, Keith's Black Magic was a terrific handling dog. Cotton told me, "If she misses that first bird, handle her quick." She was a terrific lining dog, and both Cotton and I handled her on the first bird, sometimes, in a trial, and she still placed high. It wasn't considered such a terrible thing, if the dog handled fast and well. You almost went out of your way to prove that you could do it. This was considered sharp handling.

During the '40s, the pros pretty well dominated the trials. But around

Labrador Retriever Club, West-hampton Beach, L.I., New York, November 5–7, 1948. Charley Morgan chats with Mr. Daniel Pomeroy. *Photograph: Evelyn M. Shafer.*

Women's Field Trial Club, West-hampton Beach, L.I., New York, November 12–14, 1948. Dr. George Gardner and Charley Morgan face typical field trial weather. *Photograph: Evelyn M. Shafer.*

The Gallery, Labrador Retriever Club, Westhampton Beach, L.I., New York, November 1–3, 1946. *Photograph: Percy T. Jones.*

Joplin Missouri, 1951. Charley Morgan with 4 Chesapeakes. From left to right: Bomber, Laddie's Rowdy, FC Nelgard's King Tut, and Sasnakra Sassy.

Brewster's Laddie, owned by Dr. N. M. Leitch, with Charley Morgan at Warroad, Minnesota. Charley writes of this dog: "Many people said this was the finest Chesapeake of all time. He was a little old when put in training. He had been a mink dog for a fisherman, Harry Brewster, of Warroad. Also, he was whispered to be a good deer dog."

From left to right: FC Cream City Co-ed, owned by Charley Morgan; Dual Ch., AFC Ridgewood Playboy, owned by Herb Schultz, Sheboygan, Wisconsin; FC, AFC Sage Joker, owned by Ellen and John Eliot, Brookfield, Wisconsin; Sage's Saskeram Pete, owned by Joan and Richard Kesky, Mequon, Wisconsin. *Photograph: Vern Arendt.*

'48, we started seeing the good amateurs coming along, fellows like Joe Versay and Mr. Stockwell. The Amateur Stake at first didn't amount to much, it was just for the boys who wanted to run their own dogs. There usually were about 10 or 12 dogs entered, and maybe half of those were local dogs who were running out of loyalty to the club. And it was sheer loyalty, too, for some of them to run. Later on there got to be more real interest in the Amateur Stake. It attracted some good dogs with good handlers, and there were tough tests, too.

In a handling test at about this time, a lot of emphasis was placed on the casts. You would have to handle around a bush or around a tree, so that the judges could see how your dog would cast. I remember at Manitowoc, when La Sage's Smokey won the Open, he took a beautiful cast down the river, and somebody said that he would have gone on indefinitely until he found the bird. The judges liked that. Dogs were given a lot of credit for long casts. We used to train on it a great deal. If you had a dog who wouldn't take a good cast, you were terribly handicapped, much more so than today.

Then, in the mid-'50s, the emphasis switched from the casts to the line. Today, if you get your dog in a position where he needs a long cast, you are usually in trouble. We used to line a dog straight into the water on a water blind, regardless of where the bird was, and then cast to the bird. Today we have to line at the bird, regardless of the angle.

It's hard to know just who or what is responsible for the gradual changes in the tests. Some of the West Coast judges came to the Midwest to judge, and they certainly emphasized getting back a long distance, and giving your dog an angling line into the water to see if he would continue on the line. We went through a period of standing way back from the water then.

The East Coast, it seems to me, went in for the channel blinds more. They promoted them earlier. But even though the East Coast may have given us the channel blinds, once we started on them in the Midwest, we tried to outdo them. We knew no limit to our channel blinds—we couldn't have them long enough. I can remember a channel blind down the Manitowoc River that was unbelievable.

Then, in the last five years, it looks as if the diversions, tight diversions, have become important. We almost always work the blinds in connection with marks; in the water, it's usually a triple. The marks are just a set-up for the blind. Sometimes it looks as if the trials today were decided on water blinds, and often on one particular type of blind. It looks like it narrows down to what they call "threading the needle," either between a point and an island, or between two islands. It looks like they have just about run that test into the ground. They have overdone it. I think it is unfortunate that these "threading the needle" blinds so often decide a trial.

It's not only one test that decides the trial, it's one particular part of that test—the part between that point and the island. The dog has got to be pounded off that point and driven off that island, and the fear of God has got to be in him. His entire spirit has got to be chilled when he hears that whistle, and if he even looks like he is going to ignore it, the judges almost mark him down.

There is no question that the kind of training we are doing today has been detrimental to the natural hunting ability of our dogs. I don't think hunting dogs are as good as they used to be. Of course, the old timers are always saying, "In our day, they were much better. John L. Sullivan was the greatest fighter, King Kelly was the greatest ball player, and Bill Tilden was the greatest tennis player." But I have talked to some of the old boys who knew the old dogs, whose judgment and honesty I admire, and their opinion is that the hunting dogs of today are not as good as the hunting dogs of the old days.

There is no doubt that we have better handling dogs, better mechanical dogs today. There is absolutely no comparison. That is what everybody is working on, what everybody is striving for. Today the dog isn't given a chance to hunt. You take the beginner, the amateur, his dog goes out, and if he doesn't hit the bird on the head, well, he'll run out and grab the dog and push his nose down on it. I can't see how that is going to teach a young dog to mark. I don't think they are attempting to teach a dog to mark; they are just trying to expedite matters. They don't want to spend any more time. They just want to get to that phase of training when they can teach the dog to handle. They are itching to get to the self-entertainment act, the handling test.

We used to enjoy watching a stylish hunting dog. It was a pleasing sight. But today, in a trial, it's not so pleasing any more, because you know the dog is not going to be called back.

I ran a trial at Dover, Delaware, and Walter Roesler was the judge. I thought I was right up there with one of my dogs. But Jim Cowie had Bengal of Arden—I believe it was one of the Arden dogs—and that dog hunted and hunted and hunted. Walter Roesler got up on a stump to watch him hunt, and he watched him intently. I thought that dog would be picked up, but I lost the trial to him. I asked Mr. Roesler about it afterwards, and he said, "Chuck, that was the most beautiful job of hunting I have ever seen. It was wonderful, terrific." Well, I felt kind of shocked that I didn't win, but the more I thought about the courage of that statement, and the intelligence of it, the more I admired Walter Roesler. There was a dog who had all the hunt, all the style, you could want, and when he didn't hit the bird on the head, which is an element of luck, the dog put on a hunting exhibition that could not be ignored, and was given his just credit. We know there is an element of luck in pinpointing a bird. Some falls are more difficult to find than others, and I think judges often overlook this.

It is too bad. Hunting is one of the beautiful parts of dog work, and it is too bad that the dogs are not given a fair opportunity. Of course, the time element has hurt the field trials. It has made eliminating dogs a mania with some judges. When there is a big entry, all the judge can think of is to get the dog on that bird—time is a-wasting, I have got to get through 60 dogs, it looks like rain, and it is getting dark. So his only thought is to cut down the field, and the first step a dog makes that the judge can even consider wrong, he is out.

We have gone through cycles, no doubt. The emphasis was on land for a time, then the water became more important; long retrieves were the vogue for a while, then the time element, and the increasingly large entries, caused the pendulum to swing the other way, to short snappy retrieves. Then the long lining dogs looked bad, and the judges could drool in their anticipation of what the short birds would do. We had the channel blinds until they went out of vogue, and a thousand reasons were then advanced why you should never send your dog down a channel. Who would, in a day's hunt?

Brother, a trial is not to see what your dog would do in a day's hunt, but what he will do under extraordinary conditions, judged by unusual people, and watched by an unusual gallery. The hunting tests? Nonsense! It's the freakish field trial test.

Good Mechanics

Good mechanics are absolutely essential for a good field trial. No matter how good the judges are, they cannot do a good job unless the mechanics of running the trial are good. There must be experienced bird throwers, the birds must be there on time, and plenty of birds must be available. The proper equipment must be on hand. Everything must be ready when needed, with no delays.

Good gunning is of utmost importance. In the old days, the judges sometimes used to ask the guns for long, difficult falls, and some of the guns made a specialty of this very accurate shooting. Now all we ask of the guns is to bring the birds down consistently. And good bird throwers are necessary to throw the birds properly, getting the same height and distance each time.

Back in the old days in Wisconsin, when we used to hire Joe Versay and his gang to put on a trial, we had wonderful mechanics. There were always plenty of birds and good throwers, there was no delay, everything was ready on time, and the tests could be set up fast and run smoothly.

But now we rely on volunteer help, and it takes a very well-organized club to get good mechanics. Some of our young clubs in Wisconsin have a bunch of aggressive young people, and are trying hard. Everybody is on the ball, and they generally have well-run trials. But the older clubs, whose members have put in years of volunteer work already, just can't get the help they need. Their members are busy people who can't give up the time. You ask these fellows to volunteer their time, and some of them just can't do it.

I saw one of the big officials, one of the important members of a local club, arrive well after the trial had started, and this is just not conducive to good mechanics. The important men, above all, should be on the job early. They have got to get things rolling on time.

Without good mechanics, a judge just cannot put on a good trial. How can he help but be upset when the birds are not there, the decoys are not there, the boat is not there? The bird throwers are poor, so they comb the crowd for throwers and get some poor little kid who has no experience throwing birds. It's asking too much of a judge to make him work under these handicaps.

The Purpose of the National

The purpose of the National, the World Series of Retriever Trials, is to find out which dog is the best in 10 or more series. But this purpose is fast being lost. The hysteria of elimination has become so firmly entrenched in the judges' minds that, if you have a poor first series, brother, you are through. Maybe you will be carried, but a single false step later on, and you are out.

I would like to see qualification for the National become harder, with fewer dogs qualified and running. Thirty or 35 entries would make a better National. Then all dogs could run all series, for 10 good, hard tests. No dog would be dropped, except for a completely disqualifying fault like breaking. Then the true purpose of the National would be realized. How can you tell that a dog is hopeless until he has had more bad series than there are series left to run? Only then can you be sure that this dog is totally out of contention in a National.

When the National was started, the rule was that 20 dogs had to qualify; if 20 didn't, the next top dog in the country was invited. In 1945 only 19 dogs qualified, so another dog was invited to compete. Of course, I thought this was a fine idea. They invited a little bitch with no first places, but who had a fine record for the year and was the winner of the previous year's Country Life Trophy. Well, suffice it to say that she upset the retriever world, and her handler, and her owners, by winning. This was Black Magic of Audlon.

It would be no more discouraging to meet the harder requirements for qualification than it is to know that your dog can be eliminated early in the National for a mistake that the winner can safely make late in the trial. Good dogs get dropped early in a National, and then their handlers have to stand around and watch the running dogs do poor work on tests that their dogs might excel in. These handlers, no doubt, think that their dogs could do the work the way it should be done, and they wish they could have a chance.

The purpose of the National is to determine which is the best dog in 10 series, which dog makes the fewest mistakes. It should not be determined by when he makes those mistakes, but by his total work in 10 series, or more if necessary.

Most Nationals end with a day or a day and a half left over. Why isn't this time used to give all the dogs a fair chance? I think they should plan on using this extra day. If there is a clear winner after 10 series on Saturday afternoon, fine, but why not count on giving all the dogs a fair shake and using all the time available? Only then would the original and true purpose of the National be realized.

Advice to Amateur Handlers

An amateur or inexperienced handler can do much to improve his handling in a trial. It is very important for him to work hard at it in training, to practice in a serious way. Don't take the training sessions too lightly. And don't forget, after all, that they are training sessions for the handler as well as the dog.

Marking the Falls   One of the common complaints of amateur handlers is that they can't mark their birds. I don't think any method of marking is perfect, and every handler must try to work out the system which is most successful for him.

I always pick out objects that I think are in line with the area of the fall. It is a help if you can study the background of a marking test thoroughly before going on line. Then you'll know beforehand that the birds are likely to fall in line with certain objects on the horizon or in the background.

I try and mark the first bird down accurately, and keep swinging my eyes back to that mark while the dog is working on other birds. In a triple, I want to mark the second bird also. But the last bird down is up to the dog. I rely on him to mark that bird, it is his responsibility, and about 95 percent of the time he will. I find that if I try to mark all of the birds, I may not mark any of them well. So in a triple or a double, I try to be sure to mark the first bird, or the long bird, the money bird, and keep my eyes going back to that mark—"left of the tree, right of the telephone pole." And I want to have a good idea where the second bird is.

Of course, depth perception is the hard thing. I hear so many people say, "My depth perception is bad." Well, so is mine, because we don't mark in depth, we mark in lines. But at least try to get the depth in general terms—far, short, or about half way.

In lining up the marks, when you pick out objects to use on the horizon, be sure to select things that are going to remain stationary. Cars, cows or horses are no good; the darn things will move.

I remember once, out in Klamath Falls, Oregon, we were having trouble marking our falls. It was a very foggy day. But there was a big mountain just showing in the distance, and I thought: perfect! I can line up the fall with that mountain. But when I turned my eyes back to find that line, the fog had lifted suddenly, and hell, there was a whole range of mountains out there.

So, be sure you can remember which telephone pole or tree it is, if it is the high tree, or the break between the trees. Pick yourself a good "marking post," and keep swinging your eyes back to it so that it remains clear in your mind.

A good handler doesn't spend his time "fender sitting" while earlier dogs are working. He gets up as close to the line as he can, and as close to the working handler as possible, so that he can see the test from the proper angle. Then he studies the horizon to pick out the objects he can use for his "marking posts." And he studies the field well, looking for changes in cover or outstanding weeds and shrubs to help in gauging the depth. If he can walk up on line with a thorough knowledge of the field, he isn't going to have nearly as much trouble marking his falls. He can concentrate more on his dog and handle with much more confidence.

Keep An Open Mind While observing earlier dogs work, it is best to watch them with an open mind. Just let your mind be entirely open, perfectly relaxed, like a batter going up to bat. If a batter says to himself, "I'm going to get a curve," or "he's going to give me a fast ball," he gets tense, he can't swing loose.

Don't be talking yourself into doing certain things—"All the dogs are fading right, fading right, I'd better send my dog way to the left." Maybe when you come up on line they won't be fading right any more. Just keep an open mind. You'll be forming opinions unconsciously that are fair and unbiased. And they'll be better opinions, when you get up on line, than if you had talked yourself into doing something which will be hard to get away from at the last moment. Just be relaxed and open-minded, and the right opinion is going to come to you at the proper time.

And don't be turning to the other handlers, asking, "what would you do?" "What would you do?" You'll get many conflicting opinions. Then when you go up on line, you will have a thousand ideas in your head and be in a state of total confusion. Maybe you'll start to try one idea, and then switch to what somebody else told you to do, and all in all, both dog and handler will end up totally confused. Just watch, in as relaxed and open-minded a way as you can, and kind of let things form unconsciously in your mind. Try and remember the times your dog has done similar tests successfully. Remember how you did them in training, and forget the bad times. Go up on line with positive thoughts and handle with confidence.

Of course, you'll have to take some factors into consideration. If your dog has a tendency to drift with the wind, to work away from the guns, or to pull into the guns, you'll take these things into account. But if you start allowing too much for a dog's mistakes, isn't that a mistake in itself? You are never going to get anything near perfection if you allow too much for mistakes. It is better to operate on the theory that your dog can do the test perfectly.

You certainly don't train with the theory that you send a dog way off the line to the bird, way upwind, just because he tends to drift with the wind. Many handlers forget how they have trained, what methods have worked in training, and handle differently in trials. They make too many last-minute decisions; they try to compensate too much for the dog's possible mistakes; they lose all their confidence, and put themselves into a state of nerves that is transmitted to the dog. Maybe we get a little too tense in trials. Maybe we should be a little looser at a trial and tighten up more in training, take our training a bit more seriously.

There are certain things that it is helpful to know before running a test, certain things that other handlers can tell you, such as whether you could see a dog clearly, the height of the cover, etc. Sometimes it is impossible to tell these things from the gallery. But, other than these obvious facts, it is best not to go asking advice from anyone else. No one else can tell you what is going to be right for your dog. If you ask four professional handlers for advice on a test, they are probably going to give you four different answers. They are all good opinions, but they are each thinking in terms of their own dogs, and in terms of their own selves. They all have certain strengths and certain weaknesses, and they can't help but think in terms of their own problems. So, the more advice you get, the more people you talk to, the worse off you are likely to be.

The biggest problems for an amateur come when he gets into trouble. A five-year-old kid can handle a dog when everything goes right and the dog hits the birds on the head. But when the situation gets tight and the dog does the unexpected, the handler has to think, and think fast. That is when the professional can win over the amateur, when the professional's experienced reflexes take over.

Good habits are built into a handler. It is most important to form really good habits in training, to concentrate day after day on doing everything right. Then, when a handler hits a panicky situation, when he is scared and shook-up, he is apt to do the right thing instinctively.

When an amateur gets into trouble on the line at a trial, his worst habits are likely to pop out. He reverts back to any old bad habits he may have had.

Training   It seems to me that we are emphasizing the correction of the dog more in training, and the handlers less. A training session should be just that, for dog and handler. We should take training more seriously, try to simulate trials more often in training, and do everything just as we would do it in a trial to get ourselves into good habits. Of course, we don't hesitate to correct our dogs' bad habits in training, but how about our own? We should remember that if we get into bad habits, we can rarely get over them, they will always crop up to haunt us, they are our shadow.

Amateurs, especially, should concentrate on forming good habits, since they don't usually get to train every day. But a lot of training sessions, with amateurs around, tend to become social hours. Tests are laid out which won't call for much trouble or much correction, because everyone is likely to be standing around socializing.

An amateur can improve his handling by training in a more serious way, bearing down all the time. He should try hard to simulate trials as much as possible, to be aware of his handling habits, and not to forget that the training sessions are for him as well as the dog. He should be trying to improve the team, himself and the dog, and not just be out entertaining himself.

The best bet for the serious amateur is to get with a professional who will criticize his handling and show him the proper methods. And the professional should recognize that the amateur is serious and really wants to learn.

Mr. Hasse of Pennsylvania asked me once to criticize his handling. I started to tell him what a good handler he was, but he said, "Don't do that. Flattery is the food of fools. I want to know the facts, I want to know how I can improve myself."

So we should not hesitate in being awfully frank with an amateur, a person starting out in the game, and help him start out right. Maybe we'll end up teaching him to give a better line to a dog than we can. Maybe we have fallen into certain bad habits that we can help him avoid. But I am sure that we should be very frank and very open. I'm sure that's what an amateur wants.

Common Mistakes   One of the mistakes I see most frequently, made by a lot of amateurs, is that they like to take the play away from their dogs. They don't study their dogs enough as the dogs are working. They don't let the dogs assert themselves enough. If a dog, working on a triple mark, definitely indicates which bird he wants to retrieve next, an amateur often will try to change the dog's mind, or be totally unaware that the dog has made up his mind. The dog has the picture, but the poor handler destroys it.

Of course, there are situations when it is worth the attempt to turn a dog for another bird. Maybe it is a bird in the water, fast floating into an unfavorable position. Then, maybe, it is a good gamble to reline the dog, a justifiable gamble. You can try to manipulate the dog, try to suggest to the dog which bird you want next, by turning and facing that way. But if the dog doesn't go along with you, if he doesn't accept the change, well, I'd rather give in to the dog because the dog may not give in to me. Many amateurs aren't aware enough of their dogs while they are on line.

Another frequent fault of amateurs is that they don't spend enough time selecting just the right spot to position the dog when sending for the second or third bird. There is usually a permissible area of about four feet from which to operate on line. Within this area you can usually move your dog around to keep him out of an unfavorable path, or put him in a favorable one, a natural groove. If the handler is facing that way when his dog delivers the previous bird, with his body properly positioned, the alignment of the dog's body is made much easier, and it will be much easier to get him on the proper line or off a bad path.

I think the most important things to remember on the line, besides marking the falls, are to seek a favorable spot for your dog, not trying to change his mind, and not handling too fast or too late.

Of course, the judges will tell you to handle fast, but then they'll kick you out for it. Their memory seems to be fading, but the things written in that little book last forever. Since the present trend seems to be to judge a dog on his marking and hunting, you're better off being slow to use the whistle, even if it is getting dark and there are still lots of dogs to run, or if it is beginning to sprinkle. If you handle the dog fast, the judges will love you for it, but they'll usually kick you out. However, if they do, I'm sure they will say something nice about your dog.

Once you have started handling the dog the die is cast, and you had better make the most of it. Keep your dog handling, and disturb as little ground as possible. On a marking test, if your dog leaves the area of a fall, you are in hopes that he will correct himself as soon as possible and return to the fall. But in a regular licensed trial, the time element has to enter the picture, the judges are rushed, and to salvage something, you had better handle, and handle well, when your dog drifts too far away from the fall. If you hesitate or make prolonged pauses in your handling, it seems to the judges that you don't have faith in your dog's ability to handle. It would seem that you lack confidence that your dog will take more than a couple of whistles. So once you start, your only chance is to keep at it, and make it as sharp as you can. Don't kid yourself into thinking that it was only a two-whistle job when you really should have blown five or six whistles— you just refused to handle when you should have.

On a blind, the importance of the line cannot be questioned. The quicker you have to hit your dog on a blind to keep him going in the right direction, the worse the fault must be. If there is a dike or a dam, and the blind is beyond that, I think you are much better off if you can let your dog go on a line all the way across the obstacle. If you can prove that your dog will take a line for a long distance, across whatever obstacle is there, or by whatever hazard, even though that line may be somewhat off, I think it should be a good job—a better job than the dog who had to be hit with the whistle before he reached the obstacle, who was fading away from it. Maybe the other handler ended up keeping his dog close to the perfect line, but I do not think the job is as good as the dog who went all the way over the obstacle without a whistle, even though he ended up drifting off the line somewhat. A dog should prove that he will take and hold a line for a considerable distance, even though that line may not be letter-perfect. If a dog cannot do this, I think he should be severely faulted. Some judges may not agree with this, so try to know the likes and dislikes of your judges.

The Good Handler   One thing makes a great handler: he is oblivious to himself. His dog always comes first. He is never "hamming" on line. He studies his own faults as much as his dog's, and is constantly, and with the same effort, trying to correct them. He is self-critical without building up an inferiority complex. He builds up confidence and belief in himself without being conceited. And he has enough confidence to give him poise on the line, but not so much that he fails to recognize his own mistakes and shortcomings.

Advice to Young Trainers

Please be sure that you want to be a dog trainer before you get into it. I think sometimes we create the illusion that everything is a big joke, that this is all fun. The beginner may see the glamorous side, the social side. He sees the chewing of the fat, the fun and the beer drinking. We are all having a good time. What he doesn't see is the seriousness of it, the responsibilities that we have, and how we worry about them. He doesn't understand the hundreds of hours that we applied ourselves to learning at the start. He just thinks that it's all been a lot of fun, and that we have gone along having a hell of a good time all the way.

Trainers have come and gone, and the ones who came and stayed were the serious ones. Sure, they have some fun on the weekends, but throughout the week they are working hard. And the ones who have gone are the ones who think that every day is the weekend. The Orioles are in town, the Packers are playing, and that's a good time to rest their dogs. They can always find a good excuse not to train their dogs on a particular day. But the serious trainers go out every day, whether they feel like it or not, whether they have a headache, or whether the Orioles are in town. They are working at it, hard, every day.

A beginner has to reconcile himself to the fact that there is a lot of work. He has got to get up early and work late. There is a lot of drudgery, a lot of dirty work. He has got to keep a lot of problems on his mind, the condition of his dogs, how he exercises them, how he waters them, how he takes care of them, their health and physical condition.

He has got to take care of his customers and be considerate of them. If he goes out and buys a field trial dog for a customer, and maybe pays quite a price for it, he has got to accept quite a responsibility. He can't just wash the dog out in a month's time and tell the owner to get another dog. He has got to be pretty cautious about recommending dogs—it is a difficult thing to do.

I can't always pick a winner, a good prospect. Lots of dogs who look awfully good in the beginning fall by the wayside. I think a young trainer has got to be awfully careful about this. Once he accepts a dog, or recommends a dog for an owner to buy, he has got to give it a good chance before he washes it out. He had better be awfully careful in buying that dog.

I think one of the most important points, when giving a young trainer advice and painting a true picture of the future, is that, while there may be lots of fun, lots of glamorous moments, lots of thrills, there is lots more hard work, confinement, drudgery, and monotony. If he is not willing to go through all the hard work and drudgery, if he isn't willing to take a knucklehead, or a dog with terrific faults, and play along with him, to resort to every method he knows to train him, to try and figure out new methods and new ways, to change his style and approach, to ask questions and admit that he doesn't know it all, to be willing to learn from another man by observation and by work, if he is not willing to go through all that, if the tavern means everything and his dogs don't always come first, well, he had better get out of the business. He had better quit training. He had better pick up some other profession, because, in this game, your dogs come first, they *are* first, their health and condition is primary. When you are responsible for them, you have got to see that they have fresh water, you have got to see that they have good food, and that they are properly exercised. You can't feed them one day at three o'clock, the next at eight o'clock at night, then the next day at noon, so that you can go to the ball game. You had better adhere to a pretty strict schedule, and the stricter the better.

Responsibility To The Owner   A trainer has got to accept every dog as a challenge, and he has got to train the dog as best he can. And I don't think he can ignore the wishes of the owner. If the owner wants a dog trained a certain way, even if it isn't as efficient, I don't think the trainer can entirely ignore it. Some owners are simply against severe training methods. The average professional goes to the harsher methods only as a last resort. It is certainly that way with me. I have trained lots of dogs without using the harsher methods. And I do think we follow the methods that our owners would like to have us follow as much as possible.

Some owners, I know, are simply closing their eyes to certain methods that they know must be used. Okay, but you don't have to expose them to it. You don't have to make them watch the operation. When a doctor takes out an appendix, you know he didn't do it by hocus-pocus, he had to make an incision. I think that is true in training dogs—sometimes you have got to make an incision, but you don't have to subject the owners to the unpleasantness of watching.

No Dog Is Impossible To Train   A dog trainer must accept the responsibilities of his profession and work with the attitude that no dog is impossible to train. For all practical purposes, something can be gotten out of each individual dog. Maybe the owner isn't too discriminating, and is more interested in having a hunting companion than a National winner.

You hear the statement that a retriever who has to be force trained to retrieve is just not worth it, that he'll never be a good, happy worker. This is very wrong. Force trained dogs often get into the spirit of retrieving more than those who do it naturally. I would say, as a rule, that they seem to end up becoming happier workers than the dogs who start out doing it for fun. The dog who is forced eventually grasps the idea that it is fun, while the one who starts out solely because it is fun, becomes slightly bored in time.

Perhaps a really spooky dog might not go all the way, but I have known some who became National Champions. I have had dogs in whose pens I have spent hours, trying to make up to them, who finally became fine dogs. This type of dog, the very timid one, can get under your skin, and you can really love one with affection that just knows no bounds. They love you so much and depend on you so much that it really touches your heart, and maybe your vanity. I do think that there is a little hunting ability in every retriever which can be realized to some degree by patience, study, and the right approach. Sometimes they amaze you.

Dogs don't always reveal their true personalities at first. The soft ones are tougher than you think, and the tough ones are softer. Sometimes they reveal this in odd ways. The tough dog may get that reputation because he doesn't yell when he is licked, but maybe he quits, or goes off his marking for a long time. You don't make a toughie out of a boy by babying him, you make him a sissy, a Little Lord Fauntleroy. If there is any chance of bringing a spooky dog along, it's by a close relationship. He needs kindness, but he also needs firmness.

A professional needs to keep a dog for quite a while. Sometimes it takes a long time to know if the dog is going to make it. A dog can look almost worthless, and then make great progress. It may take a trainer quite a while to know for sure; he can't tell in a month. More good dogs are washed out than are kept in training; more dogs are given up on too soon than are kept too long in a trainer's kennel.

A Gift Some Trainers Have   One of the weaknesses in our training methods is revealed by the fact that a dog's good work comes in bunches, in streaks of good trials, and streaks of poor trials. What is the explanation? It's not just that a dog is "hot" or "cold"—that much we know. But *why* is he that way?

There can be no doubt that most dogs win when the pressure is off, when they are relaxed and confident. When we are on them, they are taut, unsure of themselves. Like a ball player in a slump, they are fighting themselves. To keep a dog loose, maudlin petting and babying certainly isn't the answer. And to keep a dog's respect, continual nagging or harsh treatment can't be right, either. It's always the happy medium, a time for work, when the dog gets on the ball, and a time for relaxation, to make the dog happy and gay, to build up his confidence.

Keeping a dog relaxed and confident, yet aware of his trainer's authority, is a faculty some trainers seem to have. It's something more than giving the dog crunchons and saying "Nice dog." It's a gift that some trainers have and others might not ever have, but in an effort to improve themselves, they can strive for it. Let them give a little more thought to themselves, and lay off the dogs for awhile.

I have seen trainers who I knew were extremely severe with their dogs have a bunch of tail-wagging happy dogs around them on hikes. And I have seen other people who had miserable, dejected, cowed dogs around them, people who were kind and continually fondling and petting their dogs, who seemed to love them so much that they could not keep their hands off them. And I have thought, isn't it a shame that those dogs don't seem to love their masters.

Maybe it's because we want some things too much. Dogs sometimes are like babies in a strange group. A baby instinctively seems to want to go to the person who is not constantly striving for his attention. Maybe when we are overly solicitous of a dog's friendship, he gets suspicious.

Mistakes A Young Trainer Can Make   One of the worst mistakes a trainer can make is to get too rough with a dog just as soon as he gets him. Maybe the dog has been sent to him for a specific problem, such as breaking or failing to stop on the whistle. In his anxiety to correct that problem, the trainer may jump right into it the first week that he has the dog. He might get the problem whipped, but he'll come out with a dog who just doesn't care at all, a dog who will never really work for him.

Before a trainer gets down to serious training, he should be well acquainted with the dog. To develop all his will to please, a dog must really like the trainer and trust him, not be afraid of him. Until that stage has been reached, a trainer may be hurting a dog. At least he'll be hurting his chances of success with the dog.

You can't spend too much non-training time with a dog. Especially if it is a soft or sensitive dog, take him to the Post Office, take him on hikes, have him with you around the yard. It is a professional trainer's big handicap that he hasn't as much time as he would like to spend with his dogs, to relax with them.

So break a dog in easily and gently, gain his confidence and friendship, let him know that you are pleased with him. Just stick to the things that the dog knows, work that will need no serious correction, and that will increase his confidence. Then, when the dog really knows and trusts you, get firmer gradually. Have his tail wagging and an eager happy look in his eyes before you start putting on the pressure.

Most young trainers would be better off if they left their whips, prods, shotguns, rifles, and even slingshots, home from training sessions about three or four days out of the week. They are good to have when the right occasion presents itself, and an old, seasoned trainer will wait for this moment. But young trainers get trigger-happy. The situation may be wrong, the moment not right, when they go for the gun.

A young trainer can get over-ambitious, trying for quick results. He can get too heavy on the whip and do things that are detrimental to a dog. I heard a trainer say to me once, "I can't train today. I have a sore arm, and it's my licking arm." Sometimes I think we would all do better if we had sore licking arms more often.

I have seen young trainers get on dogs too hard and too soon, and these dogs were probably set back badly, maybe even permanently. It is a darn shame that you can't tell a trainer that. Young trainers have to learn the hard way. Sometimes, after they have gone through an initial stage of this sort and had two or three bad experiences, they are more willing to follow advice. After a young trainer has started out and worked for you for two years, you can tell him more than you could the first week.

When he starts, he has read all the books by the dog psychologists and the fireside trainers. Some of them are fascinating books. And he knows all the answers. He isn't ready to listen to a practical dog man who knows that there is nothing new, that it's all been handed down from generation to generation, and who knows that all that fascinating reading is a lot of BS. Oh no. He wants to follow a damn book by some guy who never trained a dog, but was a great writer and introduced a lot of new thoughts and new ideas because he wanted the book to sell. That's the advice he wants to follow instead of listening to you, the old, experienced trainer, who has learned from experience and long years of hard work. What you are trying to tell him has been proven to you.

One of the big dangers in a book is that the methods, even if they are more or less proved and well established, are dependent for their success on timing. Timing is a big factor, and is something that can't be learned from a book.

Importance Of A Good Helper   One of the most important assets you can have as a trainer is a good, well-schooled helper who knows and understands your methods and follows them closely. You have a responsibility to the public. Perhaps your reputation is born of patience, hard work and kindness with your dogs. Your results are obtained by repetition and not intimidation. You want this method carried on by your helper. Customers have picked you to train their dogs because you represent the methods they approve. They believe that their dogs will be happier and do better with you. Your helper must also use the same methods, or you are not being honest with your customers. Your whole kennel represents a system, and you must see that it is being lived up to.

You can't do without a good helper, one who is educated in your system, believes in it, and lives up to it. So be sure to get one who believes in your basic ideas and has the right temperament, and spend plenty of time educating him. If you can't impress on your helper that a dog can be taught through repetition rather than intimidation, and if your helper doesn't love dogs enough to be with them the extra hours that your methods demand, then you had better get another helper.

Sure we want to win, and we have certain definite ideas on how to do it. The owner of the kennel holds those ideas. If his helper cannot sell himself on those ideas, they had better agree on a separation.

A helper should be well and thoroughly trained. His actions are, at times, more important than the chief trainer's. He is in a position to do more harm, at those times, than the trainer. His methods of handling a delicate situation are of the utmost importance. There are occasions when a helper must make split-second decisions and be firm as hell. But he must use gentleness and judgement at the same time. Oh, but he must be well-schooled to handle these situations correctly.

If you want to keep a dog off an island, it's your helper who does it; keep a dog off a point, your helper does it; keep a dog in the water without landing prematurely, your helper does it. What a perfect job he must be able to do, and without putting an everlasting fear in the dog's mind, so that when the rare situation arises and you put a dog in these places, it can be done.

The boy has to be blessed with a sensible approach. He has to use his own judgement, based on your ideas, the fundamentals which he has learned from you and which have proved themselves over the years.

It's too bad if you can't sell the boy on your ideas. Either they are wrong, you are a poor salesman, or you just have a poor boy. More boys, and maybe more trainers, should be washed out than dogs. Maybe it is all a little selfish. That's the way I like it, my customers like it, and my dogs, I hope, like it, and that's the way it's going to be. I know that if you can't get a helper who will go along with your ideas, you are going to be miserable.

When The Usual Methods Don't Work   Every trainer has come up against instances when the prescribed methods don't work, and the wrong methods do.

Your dog has been delivering the bird nicely. Then suddenly, for some unknown reason, he thinks it would be a lot of fun to run away with it. You call him frantically, but he does not come. You wait, and he does not come. In your heart is murder. You go after him, and just before you catch him, he comes to you wagging his tail. Being a good, sound trainer, and following the rules of good, sound training, you do not punish him. In your mind, you realize that you are helpless, you can do nothing.

But this keeps up until you are desperate. Finally your patience is exhausted, and you take the bird from the happy little dog and you lick the hell out of him. Alas, alas, you have violated every law of good training. All is lost!

But what happens? You are appalled to find that your mistake has solved the problem. From that moment on, your dog's fine return and delivery never falters. Like Grant at Shilo, a mistake won a battle.

If you had come to me for advice when this first happened, I would have told you to put your dog back in yard training because his obedience was not completed—give him two or three weeks more of "come, sit and stay." Obedience training is never completed. A trainer returns to it regularly and continuously.

Or maybe you have this situation: your dog is a breaker, and you have used bird shot and everything else on him. But he always beat you to the bird and returned, happily wagging his tail. Since you are a good sound trainer, you accepted it—no praise but no licking, just a sour-puss reception. This keeps up, and your dog loses trials for breaking.

Again, your patience is at an end. Finally you blow your top, and grab your dog when he comes in with the bird. All the rules of sound training are violated. You lick hell out of him beyond all reason and make an ass out of yourself.

But again you are amazed at the results: your dog never breaks again. In an outburst of anger, violating every rule of good training, you have apparently solved your problem.

We just wonder how much these dogs can think, how much they understand. And also, how far they go in taking advantage of us. Dogs have been cured of serious faults by defying all the rules on how to train a dog, by methods that are on the blacklist. Unsound methods have brought results, I'll admit it. But I won't recommend them.

Problems In Training   Over the years, trainers will agree that you seldom accomplish anything in training a dog without minor faults resulting, which may have to be corrected later. The pop precedes the sharp handling, recasts precede the sure water entry, false starts and creeping precede staunchness. In other words, you rarely accomplish your goal without leaving a few wrinkles which have to be ironed out.

Once a friend came to me with a very fine bitch who was having trouble with non-stop handling. I hid Joe, the boy who was working for me, in a tree. He was a very fine shot, and he had a BB gun with him. The tree was along the bitch's flight path. As she approached the tree, I gave her the whistle, and when she did not slow up, Joe let her have it with a BB.

The next time we worked her, she was very piggy, slow, hesitant, confused. Her owner was convinced that the bitch was ruined. However, if my mind serves me correctly, she won her next two trials.

Don't worry if little seems to be gained in some of your training sessions. Sometimes it seems as if you have lost ground, but your gain may not be revealed for another day or two, or maybe even weeks later.

Perhaps an owner will say how cowed his dog was when he got him back from a trainer, how he petted him for months before he looked right. But don't forget, the trainer taught him the things that made it possible for the dog to get beyond the Qualifying Stake. He taught him the lessons that the dog needed to become a good Open dog.

Severe Training Methods   Do I believe that the use of the shotgun, shot rifle, or electric prod is brutal? No, not necessarily, if used by an expert with judgement as to the amount and time. The expert will use such aids only on a dog he is sure can take it, only when all other methods have failed, and only at the moment when such an aid is most likely to succeed.

I have been shot with a shotgun lots of times. After World War I, the Legion's favorite sport in South Dakota, where I was living, was rabbit and coyote roundups. We surrounded several sections of land and then, gradually, closed the ring. When we finally closed together in a small ring, a real bombardment opened up, and seldom did a person escape an occasional shot rolling off his hunting coat. I cannot remember anyone being hurt.

Nor can I remember a dog being hurt when corrected in the field with shot. It is not done primarily as punishment, but is associated with the training method, a tap on the rear, as the marble from the slingshot is used to make the dog sit. The shot arrives as the whistle blast arrives, suggestive of a tap on the rear, which means stop, sit. There has been a build-up, an approach, so that it means something to the dog.

The experienced trainer uses the shotgun only when he is sure that the range is close enough to be effective, yet long enough not to be dangerous. There is always a slight element of danger, but I have never seen a dog hurt or blinded. After he has felt the shot once, the sound alone is usually enough to correct a dog in the future. It will not make a dog gun-shy if the gun has been used often enough to shoot birds over the dog. That is still his primary association with the sound of a gun.

I am not a shotgun user in training. I have not sufficient confidence in my ability to use one. I just don't like to use it.

No doubt the electric prod, used occasionally on certain types of dogs, or on certain occasions such as dog fights, can accomplish a great deal. But it sure as hell can be an instrument of torture. There are people who deplore and condemn the use of these methods, who nevertheless enjoy their well-trained dogs—dogs who weren't trained with a rolled-up newspaper.

To my mind, the most brutal form of training, the one that has the most harmful effect on a dog, is constant nagging, without let-up, recess, or happy moments. That—and poor living conditions, such as flea-ridden, bad sleeping quarters and lack of fresh water, accompanied by lack of freedom, sunshine and human companionship—is what I call brutal treatment.

The professional realizes the necessity of severe training methods, and will use them on your dog only in the proper amounts, and the proper time. If his record shows any degree of success, you can rest assured that he has never failed to realize the value of reward as well as correction. A good professional weighs all the factors and applies the pressure only in required amounts, at the right time, and never in a spirit of vengeance. He is always in his stride, calm and collected.

A professional, above all, should know when and how to lay it on and off. He is supposed to be an expert, and his ability to know when he is overdoing it or underdoing it, is important. He never ignores the type of dog, and, I believe, no one likes to go any further than he has to.

No dog was ever injured by the fine end of the whip on his back end. That's where we used to get it when we didn't take to the water on Saturday night.

I have heard of trainers whose favorite method of subduing a dog and bringing him down to earth is to pick him up, hold him upside down, and literally bring him down to earth by letting him fall. It is humiliating to the dog, and if he is a little conceited, it is said that this will put him in his place. You don't have to do it on concrete; you can pick out a good soft spot.

Of course, dropping a dog off the Empire State Building would be more humiliating, and I think all trainers have felt, at times, that they would like to do just that. But I have often thought, when a trainer rushes after a dog, shrieking, "you SOB, you can't do that to me," and licks hell out of him, that he was not born to be a trainer and is taking it out on his poor dog. The secret of all punishment is that it must be sufficient to be effective, applied at the right time, and only in the right amount.

The Tone of Your Voice   One of the finest trainers and most successful users of the shotgun I ever knew had the mildest, sweetest voice I ever knew. The shot, the report and the whistle all hit the dog about the same time, followed by the sweet, gentle voice filled with assurance that nothing was wrong, "over," "back," so soft. It was apparent that he had nothing to do with that shot, it was just that darn whistle. Some trainers shout and shriek, and want the dog to know definitely that they did this, and that it happened because they were disobeyed.

I think that speaking softly and using the big club is usually the best method. When a friend gave me that wonderful book by Grantland Rice, *The Tumult and the Shouting*, I thought it was a book about dog trainers. I do believe that shrieking and yelling hurts and intimidates a dog more than a licking. It is better to educate your dogs by speaking softly. Never accustom them to being controlled by shouting and yelling, but always treat them as quietly, and with as little noise and commotion, as possible.

The tone of your voice conveys a great deal to your dogs. I went quail hunting with Cotton once. He used his bird dogs. I didn't think that anything that Cotton did was especially different, but the tone of his voice, I could tell, meant an awful lot to those dogs. When we got close to the quail it was reflected in the pitch of his voice, and the dogs picked it up. I think dogs get on to your voice awfully fast. If you go out and call them, and you are happy, you are enthusiastic, they respond to it right away.

And our unhappy spirits can also be transmitted to a dog. You wonder how much unhappy, sluggish work on a dog's part comes from his trainer and handler. As the trainer, so goes the dog, may carry a little truth. If we give up, the dog gives up. If we have no fun, the dog has no fun. If we are plodders, the dog becomes a plodder. I do believe that our dogs catch on to our spirits more often than we think. They seem to sense our inward happiness or displeasure, when outwardly we might seem quite calm.

The Story Of Lulu   There are problems, bad situations, that every trainer can get into.

A Certain Gentleman from the East shipped me a nine-month-old pup, Lulu. She was from a fine kennel, and her papers were good. We had looked forward to the arrival of Lulu.

But she came with an aura of suspicion, emaciated, and with a bulge in the middle that suggested something besides calories. Could she be in whelp? Her owner, an outstanding dog man according to his own modest admission and his stationery, finally admitted it might have happened. But, he insisted, she had only been gone such a short time that the breeding could not have been productive.

We took Lulu to the water. Her initial entries were full of zest, but after the first two or three, she suddenly wanted no part of it, and we got an absolute refusal. Just like a ball player refusing to slide, we couldn't let it go unnoticed. She was shy by nature, so we made our approach gradual. We expected her to go through a phase of extreme melancholia, and in this we were not disappointed.

We figured on making our approach very gradual and giving her plenty of time. Our record of over 30 years of experience in training has shown that, occasionally, we do guess right, and we decided to use the old, easy, time-consuming approach—nothing harsh, everything slow and gradual. We were sure that after a few ups and downs, a few discouraging and encouraging moments, Lulu would come out of it in time. And when she did come out of it, we were sure that she would regain her confidence.

But we had misgivings as to whether this Certain Eastern Gentleman would give us the time as long as it necessitated the dispensing of that certain dirty commodity called money.

Next, we took Lulu to the field and shot a bird over her. Shades of Little Gus, Hornet, Black Gum, Nip! She froze on it in a way that made these immortals just punks. This is a drastic problem and calls for drastic treatment. "Bad dog," or a tightly-rolled newspaper will not do the job. After extracting as much of the bird and as many of my fingers as possible, I gave her the treatment—a licking with the bird at the seat of her trouble, her mouth. I wanted that bird to be a mass of feathers and inert matter, not the appetizing, succulent object that Lulu mistook it for. I wanted to change it from a delectable dish into an instrument of torture—not brutally, but emphatically.

Once again, I knew that the gradual approach was called for, that it would take time and worry, and that it would again put Lulu into a siege of despondency. In this state, she just would not look good. You could even say that she was in a state of extreme distress. She was becoming a member of the old Do-Nothing Party.

What does a trainer do with a dog of this type, and all her accompanying problems? He worries, his digestion becomes bad, his nights are sleepless, and he suffers from headaches.

Things didn't work out. It took longer than we expected, and progress was even more gradual than we had anticipated. But we were confident that, if given time, we would see the light. To an inexperienced eye, Lulu looked to be at the bottom, but to an experienced eye, there was definite promise. Now we were sure that each day would see new and encouraging signs of improvement; we were sure there were better times ahead.

But before these happier days arrived, a big Cadillac drove in, and a gentleman with sunglasses and blue slacks jauntily stepped out. Shiver my timbers! It was the Certain Eastern Gentleman, who had come to see Lulu work. When he left, he took Lulu with him. You know, I believe he was mad, and when he got home, I got a letter confirming this.

She had come to me full of worms, suffering from malnutrition and vitamin deficiency, and then had seven illegitimate pups. Yet I got a letter that only a Certain Eastern Gentleman could write, pointing out the wonderful condition that she had been in when she was shipped, and how terrible she looked on her return, and that she now knew less than when he had sent her.

What will happen to Lulu? She will go down as one of the trainer's blunders. What mistake did I make? I should not have accepted a dog under such miserable conditions. And I should have been able to refuse, absolutely, to let her go until she was properly dismissed. In a hospital, people aren't allowed to walk out when they are delirious. Only under proper conditions, with a good understanding between trainer and owner, should you accept a dog.

So You Want To Be A Dog Trainer   As I said before, please be sure you want to be a dog trainer before you get into it. If it is not fun but monotonous drudgery, forget that you ever wanted to be a trainer. Don't kid yourself into believing that you can do it by kindness alone, or by brutality alone. Somewhere in the middle—patience and crunchons backed by firmness and hard work—lies the answer.

Think of the monotonous work, the confining work, even the filth of it and the long hours—not just the glamorous side, the social angle, the cocktail hour, the fender sitting, the chewing the fat. They have their place, but first, last and always—your dogs come first.

You must be able to say to your best customer, or to the biggest of big shots, "I can't join you now. My dogs must be fed, they must be exercised; they positively come first. But many thanks for your kind offer. I'm sure you understand." He will, too, and sometime in the future you may get a dog from him, or he will be recommending you to his friends. Besides, with this attitude, you will sleep better.

How Do the Fields of Training and Handling Differ?

I think, without question, that there are now two separate and distinct fields, training and handling. I think it is possible for a person to be exceptionally good in one field and very poor in the other. I think the time will come, in this age of specialization, when a man will have to declare himself one or the other. People will say, "I have had my dog with so and so to train, and when he is trained, someone else will handle him."

To try and bring the two fields together would be like trying to make a race horse and a draft horse into one animal. The perspectives are so different. Training calls for extreme patience and tolerance of imperfection—accept what you have and make the best of it. But a handler demands perfection and is intolerant of any dog who does not fit into the pattern— if he can't take it, get rid of him and get another dog.

Nowadays, a fellow can be a terrific handler, a great handler, and not be much of a trainer. He develops a faculty for working with a dog who has been trained, a dog well schooled in the basics. The dog is far advanced, but maybe he lacks a little polish, maybe he doesn't always stop too well at a distance. The man is a good shot, so he gets out the old shotgun and the dog stops. The owner comes out and thinks he has done wonders with the dog. He says, "You are a terrific trainer. What a trainer you are." And he tells all his friends about what a good trainer this man is. But he isn't a trainer. He couldn't train a dog from scratch, or a dog who has serious faults. He just wouldn't know how to go about the job. But he is a good handler. He knows how to take a well-trained dog and get him ready for trials. And he can win trials with him.

Of course, after a certain length of time, a professional handler who gets into public business is going to have to become a trainer. It takes time to become a trainer, lots of hard work, and years of experience. But a man can become a fine handler practically right off the bat.

In the old days, people brought their dogs to you to train, not to evaluate. No questions were asked. We assumed it was a good dog, and it was up to us to train him. We counted the days until the hunting season, when the owner would want him. We stayed awake nights, sweated blood in the daytime, and frequently asked the Almighty to help us. Often little was expected of the dog, but considering what we had to start with, it was a hell of a lot.

Many of these dogs would not be accepted by present-day trainers. It really is amazing how many of them turned out usable. The owners were frequently amazed, and frankly we were too. We learned an awful lot about training in this ordeal. But we were professionals; we had to do it. If we couldn't, we had no right to call ourselves professional trainers.

A person asked me once, "How does one become a professional trainer?" Today the answer would be, have some stationery printed and get a sign painted.

How did one become a trainer in my day? He hunted a lot, and showed an early aptitude for training by doing a good enough job so that his neighbors asked him to train their dogs. And he loved it so much that he could not say no. He neglected his business and maybe lost his job, but he was the proudest man who ever lived when the public gradually turned to him as a dog trainer.

In his own mind, he could train anything that even looked like a dog. It was a challenge. "Here is one you can't train." "I'll bet I can, they can't bring me a dog I can't train to retrieve, I'll show them." Little was expected, little was asked, but I never turned it down.

And what was the fee in those days? Nothing, except an official announcement at the local barbershop that you had done it. The only fee— the acclaim of the boys in the barbershop, and all the local hunters, that there just wasn't anything you could not do with a dog.

The owner never got the answer, "Get another dog. You are wasting your money on this knucklehead." We either trained that dog or we didn't train any, because that dog was going to be the only one from that owner. Maybe the dog wouldn't go in the water, was scared of birds, flinched when a gun was fired, and had no blood lines, but he was the family pet for six children. Mama, Papa, and the whole family loved him, and to tell them that he was no good, that they should get another dog, would be tragic. A $12,000 National Champion could not take his place.

They ask for so little—so give the dog extra time and patience, train him with all the loving care and affection possible, except for a few off-the-cuff blows and an occasional jerk now and then. Do it the way they would like you to, and as well as you can. These people have it coming, and besides, the dog fits into the category that 70 per cent of the dogs in public training do.

And how happy they are when their dog does something terribly rudimentary, like retrieving a duck in a pond you could spit across—and what satisfaction you get. The dog's owners will write reams of paper about what a wonderful job you did. And you did; you deserve it. So accept the challenge and go to work.

There are many more good handlers than trainers. Some of the present handlers often start with a dog who is much farther along than we were ever able to get some of our dogs. And if a dog doesn't suit them, doesn't fit their methods, they can just wash him out.

Which field do I think calls for the most and gives the most satisfaction? I think it is the lowly trainer of the lowly hunting dog who gives the most and gets the most satisfaction. He gets little out of very little, giving time, patience and work, unlimited sleepless nights and days of worry. He gets no glory, no crowd to clap and cheer, no friends to buy the beer.

Doing this kind of work has given me more satisfaction than winning three Nationals and six Country Life Trophies. I could not have done it without a genuine love for dogs and my work, to earn what I am paid to do.

Judges and Judging

What Makes A Good Judge   What are the qualities that make a person a good judge? It is hard to say, but I think a good judge has a talent for judging, and the only way you can find it is to try him. The proof of the pudding is in the eating. He has got to prove himself. He might seem to have all the equipment to make a fine judge and turn out to be a poor judge. He might not have many of the qualities that you think are necessary to a good judge, but he might turn out to have that special talent or gift which makes a hell of a good judge.

I think it's some indefinite thing in him that makes a good judge. Courage, fairness, and experience are factors, but there is something beyond these qualities. I don't know what it is, but few have it. I asked a friend of mine, a very fine trainer and handler, to name the good judges he could think of. He thought, thought, and thought, and came up with one name—the judge he had won under the previous weekend.

I don't think a man's ability to judge always depends on how much experience he has had in training or handling dogs. Nor do I think it is a question of his honesty, because they are all honest. And I don't think you can pick a good judge by how many times he has judged. Maybe he has judged a lot primarily because, like Barkus, he was "willing." In my 30 years of handling dogs, I have never refused to run under any judge, but I do feel more at ease under certain judges. And there have been times when I felt I was walking into the execution chamber.

I think that when you run under a good judge, you handle your dogs better. You have a feeling of ease and a feeling of confidence, and these feelings are necessary to a good job. A good judge wants to see good dog work, he wants to see your dog do good work, and that is his attitude. When he goes out there to judge, he wants to see all the great qualities a dog has, a dog's true abilities, and he doesn't blow some darn minor fault all out of proportion.

What if Tony did go up to the line with Cork ('55 Nat. Ch. Cork of Oakwood Lane), and Cork got up there on the line before him? Tony "came in on the next train," as it was. The dog did splendid work. It was a wonderfully judged trial that Tony won with Cork. The judges overlooked a few minor faults. It would have been darn poor judging that would not have allowed Cork to win, for the minor faults were overshadowed by great virtues. I think Cork was one of the greatest National Champions we ever had.

The better judges do overlook the minor things and really look for the big things—how well a dog marks, hunts and handles. The rules and regulations stress that. But some judges, it seems, are laying out fewer and fewer tests calling for the important qualities, even as they say that they are going by the rules.

It seems to me that when a judge drops a dog for a minor fault, he doesn't have much confidence in his own ability to judge real dog work in the field. He has got to go to the minor things because they seem to him more definite.

Maybe a judge can't help being influenced by his own past experience as a handler. He may have had disagreeable incidents when he felt his own dog was thrown out unfairly. It may be hard for him to judge that fault impartially. "When I judge, they are never going to get by with that! Believe me, the first dog who stands up, he's out for breaking. They threw my dog out for breaking."

Or he may take the opposite attitude, and not give a darn about it. Just like one judge I saw, who said, "I don't care if you yell at your dog, I don't care if you shout at your dog. I just don't want to see a dog break." Well, that's a generous attitude, but it's contrary to the rules.

These are "I" judges, rather than book judges. I would rather run under a book judge. You know what the score is, it is in print, it is the written word. It has to be easier to judge or officiate at any game if there are a definite set of rules to follow. Insisting on these rules would, I think, make judging a little easier. While we have a rule book governing the trials, rules, procedures and conduct, many judges continue to judge in a personalized way. It's "what I like," not "what the book says." I think judges should be urged to carry and study this book of rules and procedures governing field trials put out by the AKC. It is a splendid book, which some judges apparently seldom read and more seldom follow.

Judging By Elimination   The time element has disrupted a lot of the factors that make for good judging. The time problem has hurt the field trials, and it has caused elimination to become a mania with some judges. They apparently go at it with only one thought: we have got to cut down the field, so the first wrong step a dog makes, out he goes.

The judges are overanxious. A judge says proudly, "I let the dogs eliminate themselves." Well, he is crucifying the first 20 dogs so that he can give the last six or eight dogs a fair chance. I think it is an unfortunate situation.

This is the only game that hasn't a definite period of time, a certain number of innings, rounds, sets, quarters or halves. A judge can stop the game, arbitrarily, anytime he wants. Or, he can prolong it. He can name the tests, and you could even say that he can decide the strike zone as he goes along. It makes you wonder. Imagine a ball game: "Detroit was ahead in the fourth inning, so the game was stopped."

On the other hand, in our sport, "The trial was a tie after four series, so another series was added." There are, it is said, of all the billions of people, no two identical people. Of all the series run, of all the trials run, and of all the tests run, by all the handlers and all their dogs, there have probably never been two identical ones. Series can be so close, and trials so close, that after a definite number of series, it would be hard to judge. But that's the reason we have judges.

It would be hard to think of other competitive events judged or handled by elimination. Ty Cobb was caught stealing in the second inning and was dropped. Too bad, Ty—but he'll make a great dog. Babe Ruth struck out the first time at bat, so he was eliminated—but he'll make a great dog someday, you'll hear from him. Sandy Koufax threw a wild pitch in the fourth and was properly dropped by Walt. Tough luck, Sandy—you're going to hear from that dog later. Wilt Chamberlain missed a basket at the start of the game and was pulled. Better luck next time, Wilt—you'll hear from that little dog someday. Sonny Liston had a bad first round and was dropped. Y. A. Tittle's first pass was intercepted, so he went out. Say, what is the breeding of that little dog? He is the best prospect I've seen all year.

It's the only sport that has no definite time, that can be arbitrarily stopped by the judges. It's the only sport in which a mistake in the first series can cause you to be thrown out, and a similar mistake, or even a more serious error later on, may not even prevent you from placing.

What is the philosophy of dropping the dogs? One judge says to another, "I told you we had better drop that dog, or he would come back with a good series and haunt us. Now where are we?" I know where you are—you are backed up against the wall and forced to judge by the superior qualities of the dogs in the field. Maybe there are 15 dogs still in the trial at the finish, and it looks as if six could have won. Each handler and owner thinks his dog has won. The decision cannot be popular, but in my opinion it is a case of fine, courageous judging, letting the dogs finish the race instead of yanking them off the course. Judging cannot always be popular, and how popular it is doesn't always reflect the wisdom of it. I hope I am a good enough sport to congratulate the winning handler and thank the judge. If he has had the guts to carry 15 or 20 dogs to the end, more power to him. He accepted the responsibility that goes with judging. It is a tough, disagreeable job, but in accepting the job, he fully understands this. He is not avoiding the issue by elimination. He has the courage to judge.

This mania to drop dogs has resulted in the exaggeration of minor faults—"Pop, oh, I won't stand for a pop!" Even though the handler knows it is the popping of a stick that stopped his dog, the wind in the weeds, the crack of a twig, or people training in a distant field. Maybe the judge's phobia is a recast. Well, he can decide the strike zone as he goes along through the game, and whether we will play seven or ten innings.

I used to go to the trials with a judge, Joe Versay. It was not a very diplomatic thing to do, but Joe, a fine judge, was good company and a good driver. We argued, and I expressed myself about some judges. So he said to me once, "Why don't you judge?" I said, "I did, once, and found out I was no good. So I quit."

In a Derby Stake, this hysteria to cut, drop, eliminate, and avoid the responsibilities of judging may mean that the tests are over the heads of Derby dogs. Each succeeding test gets tougher, until they are not at all suitable for puppies. It leaves most of them confused and bewildered. It encourages trainers to push puppies far beyond their abilities. It puts them on the brink of ruin, and in the end, does more harm then good in developing better dogs.

Judges Must Accept Their Responsibilities   I know the terrific sacrifices that judges make, and I know what fine people they are, the hard work they do, and the money it costs them. But when you cease to try to improve the officiating in any sport, you are ruining it. All sports have their troubles, lots of responsibilities go with them, and judges accepting a job to judge at a field trial must accept those responsibilities.

The umpires are chased out of the ball park, maybe the wrestling judge is stabbed on his way to the dressing room, and the boxing judge is hit over the head with a bottle. We have attempted to improve the conditions of judging by making them serve liquor, beer and pop in paper cups. But I do think the judges accepting this horrible job should also accept the responsibilities that go with it.

It has been said that if you designate the number of series, describe the tests and the way they should be judged, why you wouldn't have anybody judging. It wouldn't be any fun any more, it would be a terrible grind, a terrible bore. This is the judges' interest, their fun. In other words, this is their pay. Well, if that is their pay, and if a judge can say, "You can get better judges, but you can't get any cheaper," well, maybe we are paying very dearly.

The popular type of judging is for the judge to say, "Let the dogs eliminate themselves." This is to cut down the field as fast as possible, and end up with six or eight dogs. To me this is not judging, it is refusing to judge. I have heard one judge bawl out another for carrying a dog when this dog later came back with a good series. "See, I told you. It always happens. Now we are right back where we were." "I am sorry," the criticized judge said, "I am a novice, and I thought we were to judge. Now I see that if you eliminate, you don't have to judge."

If you finish with 20 dogs it is difficult to judge the winner, with six or eight, it's a cinch. Of course, you don't always get the best dogs among those six or eight, and all the dogs don't have the same chance.

Of course, the time element does enter into it, and in your weekly licensed trials with big entries it is almost necessary to eliminate some dogs. But consider all the delay in deciding whom to carry, all the delay in setting up the tests. If that time were used, they could run a lot of dogs, and if the mechanics went well, they could run a lot of series.

It sometimes seems to me that some trials are more of a social event than a competitive sporting event, and that judging is a social honor. Maybe the important qualifications for a judge are his attire and the buttons in his hat.

Are field trial judges subject to much criticism? No. The only time a fellow will criticize a judge is when he loses his head, and that is a poor time. It is just not proper to criticize. Handlers are afraid to criticize— unpopular handlers have a hard time winning. Besides, the AKC can suspend them for criticizing. Maybe it's about time to go all the way and make it entirely a social affair. Then let the handlers eat in the tent by themselves at the end of the line, or in the basement. And pick the judges for their social position. As long as it is considered not in good taste to criticize the judges, and as long as the judges can determine the relative importance of mistakes, there is not much chance for improvement. Maybe the object of judging is not to be fair and to give every dog a chance, but to escape with your life.

No, it's just not considered proper for anyone to question the judging. Forget about this being a competitive sport, it's a social event, and to be asked to judge is a social honor. If you question so-and-so's judging it will hurt you, and you are not going to be accepted by the inner circle. Besides, you might be judging sometime, and then you might be criticized. Of course, you'll judge fairly and squarely, let the chips fall where they may, within certain limitations.

Yes, those who are often in the best position to criticize are the judges of yesterday and the judges of tomorrow. I do not feel as bad about poor judging as I do about the people who applaud it.

Courageous judging is not always popular. In baseball we have a term, a "homer." A homer is an umpire who favors the home team. He makes popular decisions but he is not a good umpire, and I think that would apply in any sport. In the fight between Young Stribling and Battling Siki in Georgia, the decision was given to Young Stribling at the ringside—an immensely popular decision. And then it was reversed by the referee after he got a little farther north, by phone—a fair decision. This referee just was not ready to die. He didn't want to die in Georgia, anyway.

We will always have trouble getting good judges, and no judge can be satisfactory to all, but the poor ones should be weeded out no matter how many feathers they have in their hats. I don't think that a baseball player would be a good judge of his own team; and I can't understand how a judge who works out continually with a certain group can judge that group fairly.

Why in the world would a man even want to judge? But a lot of them do. Often you hear, "Why doesn't that club ever ask me to judge their trial?" Men who complain about the hard work, about how ungrateful people are, and how unfair, say that they will never judge again, that they are through with judging and then they exclaim as an afterthought, "Why don't they ask me to judge? I am willing." They like to judge because it flatters them, it makes them authorities.

One day they are timidly asking simple questions, and the next day they are giving answers to intricate ones. They jump from rank novices to expert authorities overnight, as it were. Now they are going to determine the tests, what they like to see. They are going to determine the number of tests. They are going to evaluate them.

I think another possible fault in our judging is for the two or three judges to discuss and evaluate things too much as they go along. Why can't the judges judge separately, individually, as boxing judges do? You would get more of the individual opinion of each judge at the end. When the judges come up with the same number of points for the same dog, you wonder if one judge has not dominated the trial, with the others following in line. There is a chance for a big man to throw his weight around a little too much. It would seem impossible that all the judges—impartial, un-influenced, and with so many possible combinations—could arrive at the same figure. Sometimes we feel that perhaps we are getting only one opinion, and that if it is close, all the possible mistakes of the losers are built up, and the virtues of the winner enhanced.

Instructions To The Handlers   We have gone through many phases. There was a time when a judge would come out, put his arm around you, and would explain everything. He would almost make a Fourth of July speech. It was carried to such an extreme that it almost got to be a joke. But now, in many trials, we don't hear a thing, no instructions at all. We are sup-posed to know all the rules, and it seems ridiculous to even think of asking about them. But every judge has his own rules, and in many instances it is a sudden-death situation. "If your dog runs the bank, he is out," or "If you line straight into the water, you will be severely penalized." Only they don't tell you beforehand. You are left in the dark as to what they want, what they expect. I think we are entitled to know. When you have been months and months, even years, getting a dog ready, I think some form of instruction from the judges is certainly not out of order.

An important point that was suggested at one of the Judges' Clinics recently was that handlers should be able to mark the blind clearly. There should not be any question of where the blind is. The handler should know exactly, even if he is 69 years old and not seeing quite so well any more. This system of just throwing the blind out and letting you watch it from a different angle gives you the wrong picture. Your perspective may be entirely different from the line. It is a terrific handicap, and you are not able to prove your dog's ability as well as you would like. The handler should be able to have the confidence that comes with knowing exactly where that bird is.

Judges should be able to make everything clear to the handlers. If they have a pet peeve, the handlers all have a right to know it. Otherwise, they are just shooting in the dark. I've seen a fellow lose a trial because he let his dog ride out too far on the original line of a blind, and then, the next week, lose again because he hit the dog too soon with the whistle.

It seems there are two types of judges. There is the hanging judge, like Judge Parker at Fort Smith, who hung over a hundred men in one term of court. He built the scaffold before the trial. And then there are those like Judge Bean, who had the law west of the Pecos. He judged according to his own ideas, and the only law book he used was his own. He kept a saloon, and the man who bought the most beer was the man who wasn't hung. These are the two types of judging: the sudden-death judge, whose mania is to eliminate the field, and the judge who judges according to his own rules, his own standards, who writes his own book.

Of course, judges are our friends. They are the owners of our dogs. They make the game, and without them there wouldn't be any game. They make many sacrifices, and we appreciate them. It's this group that pays the bills and keeps the trials going, and they are not to be ridiculed by the crowd for whom they are picking up the tab. After acknowledging all the fine things that judges do and the terrific sacrifices they make, and after acknowledging their honesty and integrity, I'd like to see the professionals have the interest as well as the right to criticize their possible mistakes a little more in a gentlemanly and constructive way. This is better than going behind a bush and sulking.

The different types of judges are sometimes almost humorous. There is the judge who growls when he throws you out of a trial. "I have seen enough of your dog. I don't want to see any more of him. Pick him up, pick him up." He is almost cruel. It certainly is poor diplomacy on his part. This is a delicate moment and you are pretty sensitive at this time. His attitude doesn't make you happy.

And then there is the judge who, I always say, is preparing you for the peaches-and-cream exit. He starts telling you what a great little dog you have, "What a wonderful little dog. You are sure to hear more of that dog. Boy, you are going to hear from that dog in the National someday. What are his blood lines? I would like to have a pup out of that dog." You know he is preparing to give you the boot. You are going to hear more from that dog, and the next thing you hear is that he has been dropped. As you walk off the line, this judge probably says behind your back, "Do you think that fellow is going to be very upset when we drop that goat?"

Judges' Clinics   I think the Judges' Clinics are a fine idea for both handlers and judges. It is an opportunity to get together, to express ourselves and not pull any punches. The judges who come, and there are lots of them, expect to be criticized, and it is an opportunity to criticize in a constructive way. As a group, I am sure the judges want to do better judging. They are making a terrific sacrifice of time and money and all, and I am sure that anything that helps them is happily received by them. I think that judging has improved greatly since the Judges' Clinics started.

Of course, it would be hard to make the rule book any more concrete than it is. If the rules were discussed more, and if someone would insist that the rules were followed more, then maybe it would be more popular to follow the rules.

The real proof of how little the rules are followed came when we got to a recent Judges' Clinic and went over the rule book. Well, the number of people who have been judging for years and were thoroughly amazed at what was in the book! It was quite a confession. And the fellows who would have benefited most from the discussion were not there. The ones who stayed away probably knew less about the rules than the judges who were there, and wanted to know less about them, I'm sure.

Of course we know what's in the book, but it doesn't always come out that way in practice. If a judge is going to deviate from the book, if he has a pet peeve, he should make it known before the trial, not after.

If we could just get judges to follow the book more, if it was emphasized more, we certainly would have better judging, less trouble, and fewer unfortunate misunderstandings.

AKC Representative   I would like to see a representative from the AKC at every field trial, a man who is experienced in field trials. His very presence should help the judging. If he could watch every test and the performance of every dog—maybe even sketch them out—and not just socialize, he could be of real benefit. Then the things that have no bearing on the real work of the dogs, such as politics and the social angle, would be less likely to enter into the picture. It would also make it easier for the judges to set up impartial tests and to arrive at impartial decisions. When the pressure is on them, when they have friends running and the trial is close, it can sometimes be difficult for them to make a fair decision. Just the fact that an AKC representative is there might make their problems a little lighter.

A List Of Judges   And I would like to see an approved list of judges, passed on by both the handlers and the owners. A judge should have to prove himself, and it shouldn't take too much to keep him off that list. Owners, handlers and dogs should not be made to run under flagrantly poor judges. There are many people who have had too many unhappy ex-periences with certain judges. The record might reveal things that give the complainants a real case. The mere fact that there is such a list, and that they could be dropped from it, might keep the judges on their toes a little more. I think the professional handlers could furnish a very fair, a very good list of capable judges.

I don't know whether the professional handlers really need some sort of organization or not. If all we did was just air out a bunch of petty grievances, why, it would be a bad thing. If it ever got out of hand, or got into the wrong hands, we'd be dead. These people, the owners and judges, are in the game for the fun of it, for the relaxation. They are businessmen, fighting problems all week, and they have got to have fun. If it becomes just a source of trouble, turmoil and worry to them, they are going to get out of the game. So anything we do would have to help judging, not make it harder, and help the judges to realize that we appreciate their efforts and are only trying to help them to put their efforts in the right channels.

I know of no crooked judges. Yet, along with other handlers, I have been the victim of bad decisions, and have also benefited from bad decisions. The judges give a lot of time and money, it is a thankless job. At the same time, they are the people who are backing the trials financially; they make the trials possible. Handlers should be as considerate and as grateful as possible. And they should realize that the judges are human, and that to err is human. And handlers must also realize that, with all their intense interest in their dogs, all the hard going before, all the high hopes, they too can be prejudiced, and possibly wrong.

The handlers owe the trials to these people. But for them, there would be no professional handlers. But when they are judging, we don't like to hear them refer to the trials in the first person. "I like this and I like that. I won't stand for this. I won't stand for that. The dog is out in my book."

Your book, hell! There is a little rule book that pretty well covers all faults, and how severely a dog should be penalized for committing them.

So while we appreciate the hard work and the sacrifices that judges make when accepting such a thankless job, we ask them not to forget the trainer and handler who works for years on a dog. Maybe he has put the experience of a lifetime into getting that dog ready, and at the one period when he has that dog right, at that particular moment, a freak test is thrown at him and he loses his dog, and almost his desire to live. Then, later, he has to listen to that judge swell up with pride at a cocktail party in a cozy drawing room, and tell about that test, bragging, "I was the father of that test."

Who makes a good judge? One who believes in having Open tests for Open dogs and Derby tests for Derby dogs, one who tries to carry the maximum number of dogs and counts all the series the same, not crucifying dogs in the first series and then placing a dog who makes the same mistake in the last series. A good judge is one who will judge fairly, fearlessly and impartially, not favoring name owners, name handlers or name dogs, and— most important—he will try to avoid popular decisions favoring popular people.

Let's Face It

I hesitated about writing this book, though my friends, over the years, have urged me to do it. They felt my record warranted it. I hate to confess to doing anything to a dog but petting and feeding it. I hope you will not, after reading this, say "The brute!" I have not, and never will, I am sure, prove my ability as a writer. But my friends believe my record as a trainer has proved my success in that field, and they have often asked me how I do it.

So this has been an honest effort to reveal my methods, based on what little degree of success I have had. I have been honest—no holds barred. However, keep in mind that I hate to punish a dog. I have put in long hours,

D. L. Walters collecting much of the material for this book from Charley Morgan, in the field house of the Morgan Kennels, Random Lake, Wisconsin, January 1964. *Photograph: Walter Mieves.*

Del Huffstutter, now manager of the Morgan Kennels, and Dual Ch., AFC Ridgewood
Playboy, owned by Herb Schultz, Sheboygan, Wisconsin. July, 1966, Random Lake,
Wisconsin. *Photograph: Vern Arendt.*

avoided shortcuts, and have been known to employ extreme patience and kindness in reaching my goal. But here it goes—all out the window. Let us not kid ourselves.

What does a professional trainer use? Electric prod, electric collar, shotgun, .22 bird shot, air rifle, CO_2 pistol, slingshot and whip. Don't kid yourself, you can't get a dog to stop out in the field, hundreds of yards away, by running out and correcting him with a rolled-up newspaper Maybe you can do it in the front room at home, and then you can tell the pros how you have accomplished it with the greatest degree of perfection. But you can't take any type of dog and do it with any degree of perfection in the field, not by the newspaper method.

If the owner is embarrassed by the dog's performance, the owner gets a new trainer. The usual procedure is that the owner's wife wants to see the dog for a couple of days, or he wants to hunt with the dog, but the dog never comes back. Then he shows up at a distant trainer's kennel.

A certain type of dog, sensitive and smart, can occasionally be trained without using the harsher methods. Nelgard's King Tut, a Chesapeake field trial champion, was trained, to the best of my recollection, without my ever even going out and correcting him with a whip in the field. He was one of the few amazing dogs who seemed to love to handle in the field. I have had Goldens, Labradors and Cockers who fitted into this category. But mind you, there are very few.

Remember this, these dogs are run at trials where one or two whistle refusals will lose them a trial.

What kind of tests demand such perfection, and who sets them up? Tests that call for a dog to go by an island or a point of land where previously live birds were shot and retrieved, to skirt shores without landing, to go down channels when it would be faster and easier to land and run down the shore? At a trial, the tests are not meant to be hunting tests, or to be completed as you would complete them if you were in the field on an actual hunt. One or two whistle refusals, and you are out. What does it mean? It means that the sound of that whistle must chill the dog.

Who are the judges who set up these rigid tests, which call for—almost demand—inhumane treatment in training if a dog is to be able to perform them with any chance of winning a trial? And remember, no dog is entered unless the owner, regardless of what he says, thinks that his dog can win. Training for these tests calls for an all-out effort—shotgun, prod, electric collar, bird shot, air rifle, whip, or even the rolled-up newspaper.

Who are these judges? The owners, who never give a dog to a trainer without admonishing him first to be kind. "My dog is smart. It is not necessary to be tough with him." And on the next weekend, they set up tests that make it mandatory to be tough with him.

Sure, there are interims in training when a dog needs sweetening-up. Long periods of training that is all work and no play make Jack a dull boy, and Bozo a dull, unhappy dog. The good professional understands these things, and at the right time he will loosen a dog up, relax him with play. His professional eye will tell him the time, and how far to go. It's a degree of detraining, a recess, and cannot go too far. It cannot be indulged in until the pup is thoroughly trained.

The burden of blame for harsh treatment of dogs in training can be put squarely on the shoulders of the judges, who lay out absurd tests— down the channel, off the point, between the islands, skirting the shore. They are the last people in the world who can complain about the severe training methods of the professional. Hell, they are demanding it; the professional has no choice. And then they have the guts to say in hushed whispers to the owner of a dog who was dropped, that he had two or three whistle refusals, maybe even five or six. "See, here, look at my book. It is written down." The owner wanted some explanation, since his dog had marked well, hunted well, and had had several perfect series.

It's a pretty well recognized fact that the trials are won or lost in these tests, usually in the water. One test, mind you, and often only one part of that test, tells the story. It's a matter of survive or perish, win or lose.

What is the reaction of the handler whose dog does hit the land? The next day he gets out his shotgun. An ambush is planned on the "keep off" point. The owner had turned the dog over to this trainer because he would be kind to this dog, but he was plenty mad after the dog had to be picked up. If it happens again, he will probably take the dog away.

What is the measurement of the punishment you use on a dog? It's the amount of fear you can put in him. If you can scare a man to death by causing him to have a fatal heart attack when you say "boo," it is as brutal as killing him with a bullet. And what is the worst type, the meanest form of training? It is to put off the more severe applications, and just resort to constant nagging. I think that that is the most brutal type of training because it will make a dog more unhappy than any other type.

Maybe we could get away from these freak tests if one trainer was always good enough to be able to angle all his dogs into the water, channel them down by points, between islands, and hold long lines regardless of obstacles. If he campaigned every week and dominated the field, then maybe you would see the tests and the judging change. This might come some day—but then the judges would fault this trainer's dogs for running with their ears down, or for slow water entry, or because they "just don't like his style."

I cannot understand the man who really loves dogs and says that he will not tolerate anything but the most humane treatment. This is the doctrine he preaches. Yet, when he goes to the trial to judge, he lays out tests that make harsh training methods mandatory.

Then he explains to his friends that he didn't have time to train his own dog. He was just too busy, so he turned him over to a trainer. This man's conscience doesn't bother him, for he told the trainer not to use a shotgun, electric prod, electric collar, or whip on his dog. He didn't say this for the dog's sake, but to ease his own conscience.

A doctor once brought me a dog to train, excusing himself by saying that he just didn't have the time to train the dog himself. I told him that I understood perfectly since I had had my appendix taken out the previous year. "You know, Doc, I just didn't have the time to take it out myself!"

Now, in the long evenings, Rosie and I take rides through beautiful Wisconsin and the Kettle Moraine. She nestles close to me, alerting as always when a groundhog runs across the road, or when four teal rise up from a lake. We are happy. I think of all our trials together. She has had her wonderful moments, and some bad ones. She thrilled me at San Antonio with her back cast between a point and an island—the only dog to do it—and with her channel blinds at Madison or Duluth, her beautiful marking in the '62 National at St. Louis. Remembering all the great moments, I have forgiven her the bad ones, and I hope she has forgiven me. She, I am sure, has more to forgive than I.

The Equipment

choke collar, or chain collar: A strong collar made of chain links with rings at each end. It is slipped over the dog's head to form a noose.

leash, or lead: Use a strong one made of heavy leather or canvas, with a strong snap catch. A six-foot length is most useful for yard training. A shorter leash may be more practical at other times.

check cord: A lead anywhere from about 25 to about 50 feet long, made of heavy line or other strong material.

breaking cord: A light line, approximately 3 feet in length, made of rawhide, nylon, or any other strong, light material. It is slipped through the ring in the dog's choke collar, and each end is held lightly so that the dog does not feel he is on leash but can be stopped if he breaks.

whistle: Retriever trainers usually use the plastic Acme Thunderer or the Roy Gonia whistle.

dummy: A small canvas or plastic boat fender, about the size and weight of a bird. Some trainers like to put a scent on their training dummies, usually artificial bird scent or anise oil.

training pistol: A standard .22 caliber pistol can be used to fire blanks, or one can use a blank pistol with a solid barrel, meant for firing blanks only. Used to simulate the sound of a shotgun in training.

whip: Trainers vary in their preferences, but most use a whip made of flexible leather, weighted at one end, with leather thongs at the other. Charley Morgan likes to use a long buggy whip for certain training situations.

rope: About 75 or 100 feet long, with a snap catch at one end. Plastic or nylon is better than clothes line, since it is not as likely to fray or break.

slingshot: An ordinary slingshot using glass marbles is adequate.

CO_2 pistol: An air pistol using a CO_2 cartridge for power. Shoots a BB.

158

bird shot (sometimes called rat shot): For use in a .22 caliber rifle or pistol. The shell has number 12 shot in it—very fine. In a pistol it is used at close range; in a rifle, it is used at a longer range.

rifle: A smoothbore, .22 caliber rifle firing shells filled with bird shot.

shotgun: If it is to be used strictly as a noisemaker, "popper" shells are available which make the noise of a live shell but have no shot. If the shotgun is to be used to sting a dog at a safe distance, low-base number 8s, 9s or 12s are preferred.

electric prod: Prods powered by batteries which give a mild shock are made in several lengths. Short ones are available where dog training equipment is sold. Long ones are made for use around livestock.

electric collar: Made expressly for controlling a dog at a distance. A wide collar holds a battery pack on the dog's neck. It is actuated by a radio transmitter held by the trainer. It is elaborate and expensive.

The Birds:

Domestic, pen-raised pheasants, ducks (mallards) and pigeons are used in training and in trials for retrievers.

Pheasants are used on land in trials. They are thrown and shot. Or freshly shot pheasants can be thrown dead, both for the sake of economy and greater accuracy in the falls.

Pigeons are often substituted on land in training, since pheasants are expensive, not always available, and must be shot. Pigeons are also used for the Derby and Qualifying Stakes at some trials.

Ducks are used in the water. They can be shackled, wings and feet tied with strips of cloth which does not injure them in any way, so that they cannot fly, dive or swim. Occasionally, in trials, ducks are thrown and shot.

On land, ducks can be used with wings clipped, so that they cannot fly, but the feet are free to walk, to teach a dog to trail. Or a wing-clipped duck can be hobbled, feet tied, so that it cannot run on land.

Important Note—be sure to consult the local conservation laws before using any of these birds in training.

Glossary

AKC: The American Kennel Club, 51 Madison Ave., New York City, controls the registration of pure-bred retrievers in this country. All retriever trials in the United States are under the jurisdiction of the AKC.

AKC Rule Book: A booklet available from the American Kennel Club, entitled *Registration and Field Trial Rules and Standard Procedures for Retrievers.* All those interested in retriever trials are urged to study it. A supplement, which goes into greater detail, is also available from the AKC.

Amateur Stake: An Amateur Stake at a Retriever Trial is for any dogs over six months of age, if handled in that stake by persons who are Amateurs (as determined by the Field Trial Committee of the trial-giving Club).

bird boy: The person who throws the bird or dummy for the dog to retrieve. As nearly as possible, his throw should reach the height and distance of a live bird, which is thrown and shot.

bird-bolter: A dog who picks up the bird or dummy and runs away with it.

blind: 1. A "blind retrieve" is one in which the dog does not know the location of the bird but the handler does. The dog is sent out and controlled completely by the handler's signals. Sometimes the word "blind" is used to refer to the bird or dummy used on a blind retrieve.

2. A "blind" is also the structure, used mainly on water retrieves, which resembles the blind that a hunter uses when duck shooting. In the past, wooden blinds were used frequently in water tests, but they are rarely seen in trials now.

3. A "blind" is also the canvas cover behind which the dog and handler stand while waiting to go on line in a trial. It prevents the waiting dog from seeing any of the falls or the work of the dog working ahead of him. This is also referred to as the "hold box" or "ready box."

160

break: To leave on a retrieve before being instructed to do so. In a trial, a dog is said to break if he leaves to retrieve before the judge has called his number. In training, a handler usually considers his dog as having broken if he goes before the handler sends him.

call backs: Dogs who complete a test or series satisfactorily are called back for the next series.

cast: The direction given a dog working on a blind retrieve after he has stopped on the whistle. The handler gives the signal with his arm and voice, either a right or left "over" cast, or a "back" cast. The dog, taking this direction, is considered to be on a cast, or casting.

channel blind: A blind retrieve in water, which requires a dog to swim up or down a channel for a distance without going to shore and running along the bank.

Country Life Trophy: Now the property of The Retriever Field Trial News and known as The Derby Trophy, this is the trophy given to the Derby Dog who gains the greatest number of points during the course of a year. Through 1965, it was awarded on the basis of a calendar year. Starting in 1966, the Trophy will be awarded annually to the dog who has accumulated the greatest number of Derby points on either of the following bases: 1) during that calendar year, or 2) during his lifetime, if he became two years of age during that calendar year, except that if a dog wins it under 1, he shall not be able to win in the next year under 2.

cover: The natural growth covering a land area, such as grass, grain stubble, brush, etc. The condition of the cover, its height, density, moisture, etc., affects scenting conditions and other factors related to dog work.

creeping: When a dog who is meant to be sitting quietly and steadily at his handler's side while the birds are being shot moves forward, or in any way leaves his position without actually breaking, he is said to be creeping. Dogs will creep from excitement, and in order to see the falls better. If the handler has to speak to the dog or otherwise control him, he is considered to have broken.

crunchons: Kibbles—small pieces of dried dog food—used as a reward.

Derby Stake: The Stake for retrievers over six months of age, who have not yet reached their second birthday.

diversion: A retrieve, usually a mark and usually fairly short, which is used in conjunction with a more difficult retrieve, usually a blind and longer. A dog may have to pick up one or more diversion birds, and then pass that area on a longer retrieve without stopping and hunting.

double mark: A marking test in which two birds are thrown or shot individually, so that the dog can watch first one and then the other. He is expected to retrieve first one and then the other, remembering each fall.

freezing: A dog is said to freeze when he holds on to the bird and refuses to give it up to his handler on delivery

freezing on the whistle: When a dog working on a blind retrieve stops and sits to the whistle and refuses to take a cast—refuses to move at all, but just sits there—he is freezing on the whistle.

force training: The training which teaches a retriever that he must pick up, hold and deliver to hand any object that he is commanded to retrieve. It is usually done fairly early in a retriever's training program. A dog who has had a thorough course of force training is said to be force trained, and should make a totally reliable retriever.

gallery: The spectators at a field trial.

group work: The system of working retrievers out of a group of two or more, all on line, all steady, each going to retrieve only on his own name. Retrievers are not worked in groups at trials in the United States.

guns: Those who shoot the birds at a trial or in training.

handling: Working a dog on a blind retrieve, or stopping a dog and casting him on a mark if he needs direction to find it.

hard mouth: A dog has a hard mouth when he exerts too much pressure on the bird while carrying it. A retriever should always have a tender mouth, carrying a bird gently and never injuring it.

honoring: The act of sitting quietly and steadily on line while another dog works. In championship stakes, retrievers are usually required to honor at least once.

JAM: Judges' Award of Merit, awarded to dogs who complete all the tests in a trial satisfactorily, but do not achieve one of the four places. Formerly called Certificate of Merit, or CM

Junior Stake: For dogs under one year of age. Junior Stakes are not held in licensed trials, but are often a part of informal trials.

Licensed Trial: A trial, licensed by the AKC, at which championship points are given.

Limited Stake: A Limited Stake at a retriever trial is for dogs over six months of age that have previously placed or been awarded a JAM in an Open Stake, or that have placed first or second in a Qualifying Stake, or placed or been awarded a JAM in an Amateur Stake carrying championship points.

line: 1. The line at a field trial is the spot from which the dog and handler work. A dog is "on line" when he takes his turn to work.

2. To line, used as a verb, is to send a dog out on a straight line on a retrieve. It is a very important part of a blind retrieve. A dog is expected to hold his original line until he finds the bird or is stopped by the whistle.

line manners: A dog's behavior on line, while walking up to take his position, while the birds are being shot, while he is being sent, while delivering, while honoring, and while walking off. A retriever is expected to be well-mannered.

mark: A bird which the dog sees fall. He is expected to remember the exact position of the fall and to go directly to it when commanded to do so.

mechanics: The many operations involved in running a field trial.

National Amateur Retriever Trial: The trial, for dogs who have qualified during the previous year, to determine the National Amateur Champion of that year. Dogs to be handled by amateurs only.

National Retriever Trial: The trial, for dogs who have qualified during the previous year, to determine the National Champion of that year. Dogs can be handled by professionals or amateurs.

Open Stake: An Open Stake is for all dogs over six months of age.

patterns: The drills used in teaching a dog to handle.

pick-up: 1. The process of picking up a bird. If a dog performs the act of picking up a bird slowly, he is said to have a slow pick-up.

2. To pick up a dog in a trial is to call him in while he is working and remove him from the line.

popping: 1. Stopping and looking to the handler for direction without having been commanded to do so by the whistle,
2. Firing a gun or pistol as a noisemaker with a thrown bird.

Qualifying Stake: For dogs over six months of age that have never placed or been awarded a JAM in Open or Limited Stakes, or placed in an Amateur Stake, or won two first places in Qualifying Stakes.

recast: To send a dog on a retrieve for a second time. If a dog starts out to retrieve, returns to his handler, and has to be resent, he is said to be recast.

Retriever Breeds: The breeds eligible to compete in Retriever Trials are Labrador, Golden, Chesapeake Bay, Flat-Coated and Curly-Coated Retrievers, and Irish Water Spaniels. The last three are almost never seen in trials these days.

Sanctioned Trial: An informal trial, sanctioned by the AKC, at which championship points are not given.

series: The tests given at a retriever trial. All dogs compete in the first series. The dogs who fail are eliminated, and the dogs who complete satisfactorily are "called back" to the second series, and so on.

single mark: A marking test with only one bird to be retrieved.

staunch, steady: A dog is staunch or steady when he does not move to retrieve until commanded to do so.

style: A dog's manner of working. He is said to have style if he is fast, eager, has a quick pick-up, good water entry, and all the characteristics that make him an attractive, exciting dog to watch.

switch: To leave the area of one bird, having hunted for it without finding it, and go to the area of another bird. A disqualifying fault in a trial.

triple mark: A marking test in which three birds are thrown or shot individually, so that the dog can watch each fall. He is expected to remember each mark, and to retrieve each one separately when commanded to do so.

walk-up: A test in which the handlers with dogs at heel, the guns, and the bird boys all walk before the birds are thrown and shot, to simulate natural hunting conditions.

water entry: A dog's manner of entering the water. A retriever with a stylish water entry takes an eager leap into the water.

whistle commands: A single blast on the whistle means "sit." Repeated blasts mean "come."

Championship Titles for Retrievers

Field Champion (FC): A Retriever who has won 10 points, including a first place in an all-breed retriever trial, in Open or Limited Stakes at AKC licensed retriever trials.

Amateur Field Champion (AFC): A retriever who has won 15 points, including a first place at an all-breed retriever trial, in Open or Limited Stakes when handled by an Amateur, or in Amateur Stakes at AKC licensed retriever trials.

Champion (Ch.): This is a title given a dog who has won a championship on the Bench at an AKC licensed dog show.

Dual Champion (Dual Ch.): A retriever who has won both a Bench Championship and a Field Championship (not Amateur).

National Champion (Nat. Ch.): The title given to the winner of the National Retriever Trial. The title carries the year of the win, as in "1944 National Champion Sheltercove Beauty."

National Amateur Champion (Nat. Am. Ch.): The title given to the winner of the National Amateur Retriever Trial. The title carries the year of the win.

Vital Statistics

1894   July 29, Charles Henry Morgan born in Lamar, Missouri (about 30 miles north of Joplin, Mo.).

1912   Moved to Joplin, Mo. and graduated from Joplin High School in 1913.

1914–1917   Attended Missouri University and pitched on the Baseball Team, 1915–1917.

1917–1918   In the 32nd Division, the 147th Field Artillery.

1919   Went to Tyndall, South Dakota, in the lumber business with an uncle, and became interested in hunting and dogs.

1929   Returned to Joplin and opened a sporting goods store. Started training a limited number of dogs. Also involved in professional baseball.

1934–1935   President of The Missouri-Arkansas League, baseball.

1935   Went east for a few months in the winter to help Tony Bliss train his Chesapeakes and get ready for the early trials on Long Island. After returning to Joplin, gave up his other interests and became a full-time professional trainer.

1936   Judged the first trial held west of the Mississippi, in Omaha, Neb.

1939   Moved to Milwaukee to train at Schlesinger, Pabst and Boalt Kennels, Brown Deer, Wisconsin. Then went with R. N. Crawford, Delevan, Wis., for a while.

1941   Instructor in the Army Canine Corps., San Carlos, California.

1942   Moved to Random Lake, Wisconsin, and has been there ever since.

Highlights of Charles Morgan's Professional Career

Trained and handled 3 National winners:
> 1944   Sheltercove Beauty, Golden female, owned by Dr. L. M. Evans, Sauk Rapids, Minn.
> 1945   Black Magic of Audlon, Labrador female, owned by Mr. Mahlon B. Wallace, jr., St. Louis, Mo.
> 1950   Beautywoods Tamarack, Golden male, owned by Dr. L. M. Evans, Sauk Rapids, Minn.

Trained and handled 6 Country Life Trophy winners, for the highest number of Derby points, nationally:
> 1942   Sheltercove Beauty, Golden female, owned by Dr. L. M. Evans
> 1944   Black Magic of Audlon, Lab. female, owned by Mr. Mahlon B. Wallace, jr.
> 1945   Nigger of Upham, Lab. male, owned by Mr. Nick Bonavitch
> 1950   Black Point Dark Tiger, Lab. male, owned by Mr. Daniel E. Pomeroy
> 1953   Nelgard's Counterpoint, Lab. female, owned by Mr. Herbert Schultz
> 1961   Cream City Co-ed, Lab. female, owned by Mr. C. H. Morgan

Made the following Field Champions:
> Sheltercove Beauty, Golden female, Dr. L. M. Evans
> Chesacroft Baron, Ches. male, R. N. Crawford
> Black Magic of Audlon, Lab. female, M. B. Wallace, jr.
> Firelei of Deer Creek, Lab. female, Mrs. H. E. LeGear
> Firelei's Hornet, Lab. male, H. E. LeGear
> Sodak Rip, Ches. male, E. K. Ward
> Tiger of Clipper City, Ches. female, Nelgard Kennels
> Malarkey's Okanagon Pat, Lab. male, T. H. Malarkey
> Boar Ranch Nip, Lab. male, R. M. Sawbridge
> Chevrier's Golden Rod, yellow Lab. male, C. N. Batts
> Little Trouble of Audlon, Lab. female, M. B. Wallace, jr.

Nelgard's King Tut, Ches. male, Mt. Joy Kennels
Georgia Boy, Golden male, Dr. Irving Victor
Harbor City Rebel, Golden male, Alec Thompson
Nelgard's Counterpoint, Lab. female, H. Schultz
Beautywoods' Tamarack, Golden male, Dr. L. M. Evans
Cream City Co-ed, Lab. female, C. H. Morgan

This list contains:
   4 Goldens
   4 Chesapeakes
   8 Black Labradors
   1 Yellow Labrador

1942   Sheltercove Beauty won the Country Life Trophy, then qualified for and ran in the National while still a Derby Dog.

1945   The Gaines Award for The Outstanding Trainer of the year. This same year, twice won all 4 places in licensed derby stakes with the following dogs:
Black Magic of Audlon, Lab. female, M. B. Wallace, jr.
Black Market of Audlon, Lab. male, Mrs. M. B. Wallace, jr.
Firelei's Hornet, Lab. male, H. E. LeGear
Kiska Pete, Lab. male, H. E. LeGear